T0370048

TECHNICAL GUIDE
F-16 Fighting Falcon

TECHNICAL GUIDE
F-16 Fighting Falcon

Ryan Cunningham

First published in 2023

Copyright © 2023 Amber Books Ltd

All rights reserved. No part of this publication may be
reproduced, stored in a retrieval system, or transmitted in any
form or by any means, electronic, mechanical, photocopying,
recording, or otherwise, without prior written permission of
the copyright holder.

Published by
Amber Books Ltd
United House
North Road
London N7 9DP
United Kingdom
www.amberbooks.co.uk
Instagram: amberbooksltd
Facebook: amberbooks
Pinterest: amberbooksltd

Editor: Michael Spilling
Additional text: Martin J. Dougherty
Designers: Keren Harragan
Picture researcher: Terry Forshaw

ISBN: 978-1-83886-325-8

Printed in China

Contents

Introduction: the Viper Strikes

On 24 January 2023, an F-16 Fighting Falcon took off from Lockheed Martin's Greenville, South Carolina, facility for its first flight.

"Today's successful flight is a testament of the hard work, dedication and commitment to our customers and their missions," said OJ Sanchez, vice president of Lockheed Martin's Integrated Fighter Group, responsible for the F-16 programme, once the jet had touched down after its 50-minute flight. "This milestone demonstrates Lockheed Martin's commitment to advancing this programme and getting this much-needed aircraft and its advanced 21st-century security capabilities to the warfighter."

The aircraft that made its maiden flight from Greenville, home of a new production line for the aircraft, was one of more than 4,500 F-16s that have been manufactured for 26 nations around the globe and counting. But it was also the first F-16 Block 70 to take to the air.

This latest Block 70 configuration includes such innovative features as an active electronically scanned array (AESA), the Northrop Grumman AN/APG-83 that provides pilots with enhanced situational awareness, flexibility and quicker all-weather targeting, as well as highly detailed imagery of the target area and digital map displays. There's also a new, high-resolution Centre Pedestal Display (CPD), providing pilots with critical tactical imagery, including that derived from the AESA radar and targeting pods.

Items such as these would have been entirely alien to the test pilots who began putting the original YF-16 prototype aircraft through their paces, starting with an (unplanned) first flight on 20 January 1974, during a high-speed taxi test.

Revolutionary design

But the fact that the Block 70/72, the latest new-build iteration of the F-16, is still in such demand today – with a backlog of 128 jets in the order book, as of early 2023 – demonstrates the excellence of the original design, which first received a production order back in 1975.

The F-16 was conceived at the height of the Cold War and with the air combat lessons of the Vietnam War firmly in mind. At the outset, its design stressed simplicity, light weight and a high degree of manoeuvrability. As such, it was a radical alternative to the increasingly sophisticated, heavy and un-manoeuvrable combat jets that were, at this time, the order of the day.

The Fighting Falcon was, when it appeared, a revolutionary breakthrough in fighter design.

Key features included a smooth blended wing/body that generated considerable extra lift and control and a pioneering fly-by-wire control system that ensured stability while also increasing agility. The F-16's pilot was provided with a slightly tilted back ejection seat, a side-mounted control stick, head-up display and a bubble canopy providing excellent visibility. All these characteristics can still be found on the latest F-16s being built today.

As it was, however, the idea of the F-16 as an 'austere' day fighter designed to do battle with Warsaw Pact jets in a future East–West confrontation over the Central Front quickly got overtaken. All the same, the F-16 has long been one of the most agile and capable dogfighters of its generation.

Even with the service entry of increasing numbers of fifth-generation F-35 Joint Strike Fighters – designed to replace vast numbers of F-16s, among others – there is still very much a place for an advanced, fourth-generation warplane like the Fighting Falcon.

As well as continuing to add advanced new capabilities to the basic design, Lockheed Martin has also employed other strategies to ensure the continued popularity of the F-16 – more than 3,000 of which are operating today in 25

countries. The Fighting Falcon has long been prized for its affordable lifecycle costs, a legacy of the low-cost fighter concept from which it originally stemmed. Lockheed Martin (and General Dynamics before it) has also been willing to forge regional and worldwide partnerships, which has seen production and licensed assembly take place in different countries around the world, establishing a global supply chain concept that is also now integral to the F-35 programme.

Combat tested

In the course of at least 13 million sorties, F-16s have flown around 19.5 million flight hours, many of them in combat or otherwise on operational duty. Many of the F-16's operators have taken the F-16 to war, with considerable success, starting with Israel, which scored the first of many air-to-air kills with the Fighting Falcon over Lebanon's Bekaa Valley in April 1981.

With the US Air Force (USAF), the F-16 has always been in the shadow of the highly-capable F-15 Eagle when it comes to air-to-air missions, but it has instead established itself as a 'mud-mover' par excellence. The Fighting Falcon's combat debut with the USAF came during Operation Desert Storm in 1991, when more missions were flown by F-16s

BAHRAINI AIR FORCE F-16
A Royal Bahraini Air Force F-16 Block 70 aircraft flies above Edwards Air Force Base, California, March 2023.

than any other aircraft. During the US Air Force's first war in Iraq, the F-16 excelled in missions that included attacking airfields, military production facilities and missile sites. At this time, the range of precision-guided munitions available to the F-16, and its night- and poor-weather fighting capabilities, were very much lacking. It was only after Desert Storm, during an air-policing mission, that a US Air Force F-16 finally scored that service's first air-to-air 'kill' with the type – an Iraqi MiG-25 Foxbat was the victim.

In the years since, considerable efforts have been made to make the F-16 a more potent fighter for both air-to-air and air-to-ground missions. More powerful weapons and sophisticated targeting systems were added, so that the latest F-16 Block 70/72 is equally proficient at flying long-range precision strike missions as it is defending airspace with its AESA radar and beyond-visual-range air-to-air missiles. Remarkably, more than 3,300 carriage and release configurations have been certified for the F-16 across its service career, involving more than 180 different weapons and stores.

The F-16 is therefore heading into the third decade of the 21st century in excellent shape and with a long period of service still ahead of it.

Opposite: PILOT TRAINING
Captain Zoe Kotnik, a 55th Fighter
Squadron pilot from Shaw Air Force
Base, S.C., clips on her mask in
her F-16 Fighting Falcon prior to a
training sortie, November 2017.

Below: BUBBLE CANOPY
Its bubble canopy and wingtip
armaments prominent, an F-16C from
the 138th Fighter Wing, Tulsa Air
National Guard (ANG), flies behind a
KC-135R Stratotanker for refuelling
during flight operations over Kansas.

Origins and LWF

The origins of the F-16, the most popular Western fighter aircraft of the modern era, date back to the hard lessons learned by the US Air Force in the Vietnam War. The latest versions of the F-16 are true multirole warplanes, able to perform air-to-air and air-to-ground missions with equal efficiency and in all weathers, and they also regularly carry significant amounts of weapons, fuel, targeting pods and other stores.

COMBAT PATROL

A US Air Force F-16CJ assigned to the 555th Fighter Squadron, armed with AIM-120 Advanced Medium Range Air-to-Air Missiles (AMRAAM), GBU-12 500-pound bombs, and a GBU-31 Joint Direct Attack Munitions (JDAM), flies over Iraq during Operation Enduring Freedom, 2003.

As first envisioned, the F-16 was very much a throwback to the generation of fighters that came before the long-running war in Southeast Asia. The initial concept for the F-16 was a low-cost and somewhat unsophisticated aircraft with a single seat and engine. At the time, this flew in the face of the trend for ever larger and more complex fighters, often two-seaters, with a pilot and weapons systems officer and the capacity to undertake a wide range of missions.

Typical of these larger warplanes was the McDonnell Douglas F-15 Eagle, designed to ensure the dominance of the US Air Force against the latest Soviet aircraft of the day. The size and payload of the F-15 meant that it was equally suitable for long-range strike and battlefield interdiction, as well as its primary role of air dominance. But all this capability came at a significant cost, and the F-16, at least initially, was intended to be a much less expensive option.

Advanced Day Fighter
The first studies into the kind of low-cost, high-performance day fighter that would later result in the F-16 began in 1965. At this point, the US Air Force began looking at an Advanced Day Fighter (ADF), initially intended to weigh only 11,340kg (25,000lb). Combined with a powerful engine, this would yield an excellent thrust-to-weight ratio and high wing loading. The agility of the F-16 has always been one of its hallmarks. However, at this early stage, it was very much seen as a means of achieving dominance over the MiG-21 – at that time the pre-eminent lightweight fighter used by the Soviet Union, its Warsaw Pact allies and many other operators around the world.

In the mid-1960s, the US Air Force was dominated by the McDonnell Douglas F-4 Phantom II, and it was also beginning to introduce the General Dynamics F-111. Both of these, to varying degrees, were big, heavy and complex designs that required a considerable amount of maintenance. Each also had twin engines and a crew of two. In the skies over Vietnam, it became clear that the design philosophy behind the F-4 was not necessarily suitable to take on smaller and more agile foes like the MiG-21.

While the ADF promised to turn the tables on the MiG-21 and to have much reduced procurement and operating costs

VIETNAM WAR SERVICE
A US Navy Phantom F4B fires rockets at ground targets during an attack on a Viet Cong position, South Vietnam. The F-4 Phantom was the maintstay of the US Navy and US Air Force during the 1960s and 1970s.

compared to those of the F-4 (to say nothing of the F-111), the US Department of Defense was unconvinced. The appearance of the MiG-25 – a much larger and more complex fighter than the MiG-21, and with a performance that outstripped its contemporaries – led to a rethink of priorities. For the proponents of larger and more sophisticated fighters, the MiG-25 provided suitable ammunition to shoot down the ADF concept – at least for now.

F-X fighter

While the appearance of the MiG-25 in 1967 provided a scare, the demise of the ADF study did not mean that the lightweight fighter idea was entirely dead within the United States.

In 1966–67, the Pentagon began to look at the F-X fighter study, which again examined the potential of a lower-cost tactical jet. With the demands of the Vietnam War very much in mind, it seemed that the F-X could offer a means of bolstering the US Air Force tactical fleet for relatively little expenditure. In the event, the service instead received the Vought A-7 Corsair II, an adapted naval attack aircraft purchased off-the-shelf to meet emerging air-to-ground requirements in Southeast Asia. It would prove to be another false start for the lightweight fighter concept.

In 1969, the Pentagon, with concerns around the overall sizes of US tactical fighter fleets still on its mind, issued an air power

memorandum that recommended buying a lightweight F-XX fighter as a cheaper alternative to the US Air Force's F-15 and the US Navy's Grumman F-14 Tomcat, both of which were then still in development. The Pentagon believed that such a move could lead to a doubling of the tactical fighter inventories of both services.

However, there was now resistance from within both the US Air Force and Navy, neither of which were willing to compromise their planned F-14 and F-15 fleets, these aircraft being seen (with some justification) as necessary to counter the pace of development of new fighters in the Soviet Union.

Before the end of the decade, however, the lightweight fighter had gained some significant support in the shape of Deputy Defense Secretary David Packard. Packard not only supported the

proposition of a more austere fighter, but he also promoted the idea of using rapid prototyping to test potential new aircraft designs before placing any large-scale orders. At this time, there were a few potential designs that could have met such a requirement, including the Lockheed CL-1200, the Northrop P-350 Cobra and the Vought V-1100. Within the US Air Force and industry, there was also still interest in getting a 'no-frills' fighter design of this kind into service.

It was Packard who would play an influential role in kickstarting the Lightweight Fighter (LWF)

DAVID PACKARD
Chairman of the President's Committee on Defense Management David Packard speaks at a press briefing. He was a leading supporter of the Lightweight Fighter (LWF) programme.

program that would eventually lead to the F-16.

Lightweight Fighter (LWF) Program

On 6 January 1972, a request for proposals (RFP) was issued to industry calling for potential LWF designs. The LWF was, in some ways, a throwback to the previous F-XX concept, which had been promoted above all by the influential defence analyst Pierre Sprey. Working at the Pentagon, Sprey was part of the self-styled 'Fighter Mafia', which pushed for high-energy, high-manoeuvrability fighter designs as a counterweight to heavy and complex aircraft like the F-15.

LWF inherited several design requirements from F-XX, including a high thrust-to-weight ratio, excellent manoeuvrability, a load factor of 6.5g (0.23oz) and an optimum gross weight of 9072kg (20,000lb).

Proposals for the LWF were received from five different manufacturers, and in March 1972, the Boeing Model 908-909 was selected by the Air Staff as the preferred option. The next best options were determined to be the General Dynamics Model 401 and the Northrop P-600.

Evaluation work continued, and ultimately, the Source Selection Authority, under Lt Gen James Stewart, determined that the General Dynamics and Northrop proposals were preferable to the Boeing design. A final decision approving this move was then made by Secretary of the Air Force Robert C. Seamans. This meant that the LWF effort could now move towards the full-scale prototype stage. These prototypes would emerge as the General Dynamics YF-16 and the Northrop YF-17.

YF-16 prototype

At the helm of the General Dynamics design team for the YF-16 was Harry J. Hillaker. He oversaw the study of dozens of different configurations for austere fighters, starting with the FX-404 study that first emerged in the mid-1960s and leading up to the Models 785, 786 and 401. It was the last of these that was further refined to become the YF-16, and, for its time, its appearance and design philosophy

YF-16 PROTOTYPE
12 October 1973: the new lightweight YF-16 is unveiled by the General Dynamics team.

YF-16 CONTROL CONFIGURED VEHICLE (CCV)

The first YF-16 prototype (serial number 72-1567) was rebuilt in December 1975 to become the US Air Force Flight Dynamics Laboratory's Control Configured Vehicle (CCV). The primary change to the airframe was a prominent pair of canted canard fins splayed outwards in an inverted-V configuration below the engine air intake. Other changes included modified flight controls that allowed the use of the wing trailing-edge flaperons in combination with the all-moving stabilator. The fuel system was also adapted so that fuel could be transferred from one tank to another to change the aircraft's centre of gravity.

In this form, the YF-16 CCV was used for decoupled manoeuvring trials, in which the aircraft manoeuvres in one plane but without movement in another. For example, the aircraft could turn without having to bank. A key element

COCKPIT CONTROLS
A YF-16 aircraft cockpit, shown here at Edwards Air Force Base, California.

of the programme was testing the aircraft's ability to point its nose in one direction without having to change its flight path. This kind of high-angle manoeuvring would later be further explored by the F-16 AFTI (Advanced Fighter Technology Integration) test aircraft as well as the purpose-built Rockwell X-31. It is now a fundamental part of the design ethos for highly manoeuvrable fighter aircraft such as the Lockheed F-22 Raptor.

The YF-16 first flew after its CCV modifications on 16 March 1976, and it completed 87 sorties before the end of the test programme on 31 July 1977.

were no less than radical. As part of the 'Fighter Mafia', perhaps it was no surprise that Hillaker's Model 401-16B as originally schemed was an extremely austere day fighter. Lacking even a radar, it was armed with a single 20mm (0.79in) M61A1 rotary cannon and short-range infrared-homing AIM-9 Sidewinder air-to-air missiles. Befitting the concept of a MiG-21 killer, the design of what became the F-16 was optimized for 'turn and burn' aerial engagements, as well as air-to-air combat at altitudes of 9144–12,192m (30,000-40,000ft) and speeds of Mach 0.6–1.6 or 741–1976km/h (460–1228mph).

From the start, the F-16's cockpit was designed to incorporate a sidestick controller rather than a traditional central joystick. The sidestick was mounted on a console to the right of the pilot and has remained a feature of the aircraft, and its many variants, ever since.

In terms of avionics, the F-16 boasted 'fly-by-wire' (FBW) flight controls, becoming one of the first aircraft to feature this computer-controlled system that helps manage all aspects of its in-flight behaviour. The FBW system ensured that the aircraft did not depart controlled flight, even when the pilot was demanding the highest levels of manoeuvrability (for example, during a dogfight).

On the outside, the F-16 also introduced some unusual features, including the distinctive low-slung engine air intake and the 'blended' merge between the wing and the fuselage. The prominent cockpit canopy is another distinguishing feature. This, combined with the pilot's high-up position despite the reclined ejection seat, provides superb all-round vision especially useful in close-quarters air combat.

First tests

The first prototype YF-16 was rolled out of the General Dynamics facility in Fort Worth, Texas, on 13 December 1973. It was then

YF-16 AND YF-17
An air-to-air right side view of a YF-16 and a YF-17 aircraft, side-by-side, armed with AIM-9 Sidewinder air-to-air missiles.

loaded into a Lockheed C-5 Galaxy transport and flown to Edwards Air Force Base, the California-located hub of the US Air Force's flight test community. The Galaxy and its YF-16 touched down at the base on 8 January 1974.

The first flight of the YF-16 was unplanned. On 20 January 1974, during a high-speed taxi test, test pilot Phil Oestricher encountered a rolling divergent oscillation. This led to the prototype's right horizontal stabilizer contacting the runway. With no other obvious means of countering this, Oestricher decided "to fly out of the situation".

An official first flight, with a duration of 90 minutes, took place at Edwards Air Force Base on 2 February 1974, with Oestricher again at the controls.

The first flight of the second prototype (72-01568) followed on 9 May 1974, this time with

test pilot Neil Anderson in the cockpit. There followed a period of extensive flight tests comparing the YF-16 and the YF-17 and involving large numbers of pilots. In the process of this competitive fly-off, the jets were also flown against the US Air Force's own secret fleet of Soviet-made MiG-17 and MiG-21 fighters. These fighters were operated out of Tonopah Test Range Airport, Nevada, by a unit known as the Red Hats.

On 13 January 1975, Air Force Secretary Dr John L. McLucas announced that the YF-16 had been chosen ahead of the YF-17 for the US Air Force's LWF requirement. In its favour (among other factors) was its unit cost – around $250,000 less than that of an F-17. The General Dynamics entrant was also judged to be cheaper to operate and to have a longer range and superior manoeuvrability.

YF-17 TEST FLIGHT
The Northrop Aviation YF-17 technology demonstrator aircraft in flight during a 1976 flight research program at NASA's Dryden Flight Research Center, Edwards Air Force Base, California. The objectives of the seven-week flight test programme included the study of manoeuverability of this aircraft at transonic speeds and the collection of in-flight pressure data from around the afterbody of the aircraft to improve wind-tunnel predictions for future fighter aircraft. All 25 research flights were full-data flights. They obtained data on afterbody pressures, vertical-fin dynamic loads, agility, pilot physiology and infrared signatures. The average flight time was 45 minutes.

All was not lost for the Northrop design, however, with the YF-17 going on to form the basis of the US Navy's carrier-capable F/A-18 Hornet.

Long service

The basic excellence of Hillaker and his team's F-16 design has meant that the aircraft that remains in production to this day looks almost identical to the original prototype first flown back in 1974. In the meantime, the manufacturer and the production facility have changed, and the spectrum of missions that the aircraft can undertake is probably beyond what Hillaker ever imagined.

The early models of the F-16 that entered service at the beginning of the 1980s were broadly in keeping with the original lightweight fighter doctrine. Although these aircraft arrived with a radar, their primary armament for air-to-air missions remained the internal M61A1 cannon and infrared-homing AIM-9 Sidewinder missiles – there was no capacity for them to launch beyond-visual-range air-to-air missiles, in the beginning, at least.

It did not take long, however, for the US Air Force and its NATO allies to press the new fighter into service for air-to-ground missions as well. In this way, the F-16 began the long journey to becoming a notably robust, multirole warplane, and ultimately one with a high level of precision attack capability. Much of this was inevitable, especially since the US Air Force, which regularly deploys its forces considerable distances around the globe, has never really had a huge requirement for a truly lightweight fighter (other than in specific localized conflicts). And with the demand to replace a variety of different fighter and attack jets, both within the US Air Force and with its many allies, it soon became clear that the highly adaptable, ever-dependable F-16 was in many ways the ideal solution to supersede all manner of different combat aircraft. In this way, the F-16 took the place of types ranging from the heavyweight F-4 of the Vietnam era to the lightweight Northrop F-5 that was widely exported to US allies, and even highly specialized types like the Fairchild A-10 Thunderbolt II attack aircraft.

MODELLING

A YF-16 model is prepared for testing in a 2.4 x 1.8 metre (8 x 6 ft) Supersonic Wind Tunnel.

SWEPT-FORWARD WING DESIGN

In the mid-1970s, the potential offered to fighters by a swept-forward wing began to be studied more seriously. Above all, this unorthodox configuration promised to reduce drag and enhance low-speed handling characteristics. Until this point, however, projects of this kind had been hampered by manufacturing limitations since swept-forward wings were notoriously difficult to produce using conventional techniques.

In 1976, the Defense Advanced Research Projects Agency (DARPA) organization awarded funds to General Dynamics, Rockwell and Grumman to study swept-forward wings on tactical aircraft. The programme was enabled by advances in manufacturing techniques largely surrounding the new types of advanced composite materials that ensured the wing was rigid enough to cope with the rigours of aerodynamic stress yet light enough to not adversely affect flight characteristics and

X-29 DEMONSTRATOR
The No.2 X-29 technology demonstrator aircraft is seen here during a 1990 test flight. At this angle, the aircraft's unique forward-swept wing design is clearly visible.

performance. The General Dynamics design team looked at several different swept-forward wing design variations based on the F-16 including one with canard foreplanes and an aft-mounted wing. The company ultimately settled on a slightly lengthened and strengthened fuselage to accommodate a swept-forward wing that was slightly larger than the standard wing.

In January 1981, DARPA selected the rival Grumman 712 instead of the General Dynamics offering, and this winning design later became the X-29A. While no F-16 with swept-forward wing was ever completed, the successful X-29A itself incorporated some elements of the F-16, including its fly-by-wire flight control system.

F-16A/B: The First Generation

After the prototype YF-16s, General Dynamics progressed to building a batch of eight Full-Scale Development (FSD) aircraft completed to the original F-16A (single-seat) and F-16B (two-seat) standards. The first of the FSD aircraft, an F-16A, took to the air at the company's plant in Fort Worth, Texas, on 8 December 1976. These early production airframes featured black-painted radomes that would eventually give way to light grey on later production aircraft. Another distinguishing feature was the black radar warning receivers (RWR) on either side of the fuselage.

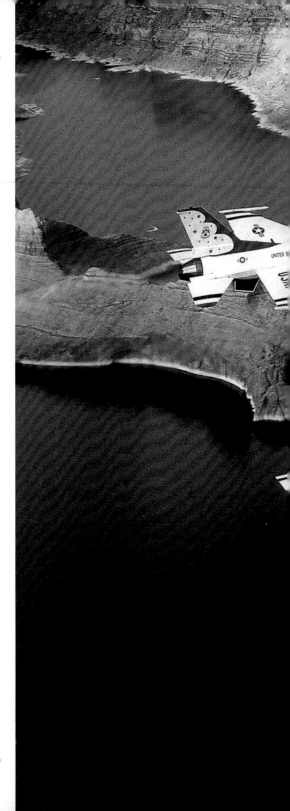

THUNDERBIRDS ARE GO
The USAF Air Demonstration Squadron fly in formation. The General Dynamics F-16A Fighting Falcons on display were the first F-16s to be received by the Thunderbirds in 1982 when they transitioned from T-38s to F-16 aircraft.

As discussed in the previous chapter, the original proposal for an 'austere' day fighter had been abandoned by this stage, with the F-16A/B coming off the production line with a Westinghouse AN/APG-66 radar.

Significant changes over the prototypes included a fuselage stretch, providing a length of 15.09m (49ft 6in) and a fin height of 5.08m (16ft 8in). Those dimensions were common to both the F-16A and F-16B, with the two-seater also retaining the same weight while not adding more aerodynamic drag. Compared

MISSILE LAUNCH
A left-sided view of an F-16B Fighting Falcon firing an AGM-45 Shrike anti-aircraft missile over the Edwards Air Force Base Test Range, California.

to the single-seater, however, the F-16B had reduced internal fuel capacity, with 580kg (1,500lb) less fuel. Primarily, the FSD aircraft were used to continue testing the F-16 ahead of its service entry, although the third and fifth F-16As from this batch were ultimately modified to become F-16XL aircraft with an entirely new 'cranked arrow' delta wing.

Block 1
The initial production batch of F-16A/B aircraft, known as Block 1, provided a broadly similar standard to the Full-Scale Development airframes. They also retained the black radomes and RWRs. The power plant was the Pratt & Whitney F100-PW-200 turbofan engine. While the Block 1 designation covered both single-seaters and two-seaters, surviving

aircraft – together with those from the subsequent Block 5 production run – were subsequently brought up to Block 10 standard with minor equipment changes, this work occurring from 1982–84.

The Block 5 aircraft were the first to introduce grey-painted radomes and RWR fairings, which then became standard on subsequent airframes. These F-16A/Bs also retained the F100-PW-200 turbofan.

The Block 10 aircraft were broadly similar but featured some minor internal changes. Specific derivatives based on the Block 10 included a batch of 24 aircraft adapted for the ground-attack role under the Pave Claw programme as well as several jets that were converted to become ground instructional airframes under the GF-16A designation.

F-16XL

TEST FLIGHT
General Dynamics
F-16XL (serial number
75-0749) on its first test
flight over the Texas
countryside, flown by test
pilot James A. McKinney.

Few, if any, F-16s underwent such a radical reconfiguration as the F-16XL version, with its entirely new 'cranked-arrow' delta wing. Originally proposed by the manufacturer in 1980, the new wing for the F-16XL was developed by General Dynamics in collaboration with NASA and was influenced by studies that showed how this planform minimized drag across the transonic and supersonic regimes.

As well as the new wing, the fuselage of the F-16XL was modified, being increased in length via the insertion of two separate plugs. The ventral fins were also deleted from the two F-16XLs, which were created by modifying the third and fifth F-16As from the FSD batch. The drag-reducing benefits of the delta wing were combined with a significant increase in external load-carrying capacity. In all, the F-16XL had a remarkable 17 hardpoints across the underside of its wing, providing a total of 29 separate external stores stations. These stations included semi-recessed carriage for four AIM-120 AMRAAMs along the wing roots, plus two more of these missiles (or AIM-9 Sidewinders) on the wingtips.

The first F-16XL, a single-seater, took to the air on 15 July 1982 and was followed into the air by the second example, which was converted as a two-seater, later the same year. In 1982 the US Air Force had launched its Dual-Role Fighter (DRF)

competition that aimed to find a replacement for the General Dynamics F-111 as well as F-4 Phantoms serving in the long-range strike role. Had the F-16XL been chosen, it would have become the F-16E (single-seat) and F-16F (two-seat) – designations that were later reused for the Block 60 Desert Falcon aircraft ordered by the United Arab Emirates. In the event, the US Air Force opted for the F-15E Strike Eagle. The F-16XL was not judged markedly inferior to the F-15E, but it was determined that the General Dynamics design would cost more to develop and manufacture, that it had reduced growth potential and a projected higher attrition rate.

The F-16XL's job was not done, however, and the delta-wing jet continued to be used for a variety of experimental roles. In 1989, the single-seat F-16XL had a portion of its left wing replaced with a section of titanium with millions of laser-cut holes, to test the effects of the turbulent airflow over the surface of the wing. Both the F-16XLs were also used for studies into take-off performance and engine noise effects, as well as separate tests involving laminar flow and vortex flaps. In 1998, the single-seat F-16XL was also fitted with an entirely new Digital Flight Control System (DFCS), equivalent to that fitted to the Block 40 aircraft, and completed 10 test flights in this configuration.

ALTERNATIVE ENGINES: F-16/79 AND F-16/101

From the start it was clear that the F-16 would generate considerable interest on the export market, although as an advanced fighter that was being delivered to frontline US Air Force units there was initially some concern about whether it was suitable for certain nations, based on political sensitivities.

This was a particular issue after President Jimmy Carter introduced a more restrictive arms export policy in 1977. Among its provisions was that foreign nations should not be able to receive combat aircraft that were as capable as those being produced for domestic operators.

General Electric J79
This state of affairs led to the development of the F-16/79, the primary change being the replacement of the Pratt & Whitney F100 engine with the General Electric J79. This previous-generation turbojet already powered the F-104 Starfighter and the F-4 Phantom II, both of which were well established as export products. Introducing the J79 engine into the F-16 required a reworked rear fuselage, with a distinctive extended tailpipe. The prototype F-16/79 was a two-seater, with the J79-GE-119 engine, a variant specific to the Fighting Falcon.

In the event, the export-configured F-16/79 failed to win any orders and it was soon rendered obsolete by a change in arms export policy, implemented by President Carter in 1980. The situation for prospective export customers was then relaxed further still once President Ronald Reagan took office in 1981. With this, potential foreign customers were able to buy the standard F-16A/B instead.

F-16/101
Another early F-16 version with a different powerplant to the original F-16A/B was the F-16/101, with some changes to the tailpipe and the air intake, to accommodate the General Electric YJ101 two-shaft augmented turbojet. In this capacity, the F-16/101 served as the testbed for the future F110-engined F-16 variants, a process that took place under the Alternative Fighter Engine (AFE) programme. The F110 would eventually find a place on the F-16 beginning with the Block 30 production aircraft, followed by the Block 40, Block 50, and so on.

F-16/79
On 29 October 1980, F-16/79 (No. 50752) intermediate fighter prototype made its maiden flight, piloted by James A. McKinney.

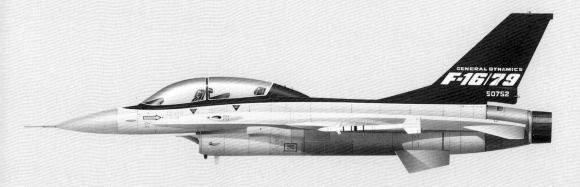

F-16A Block 15B ADF

Weight (maximum take-off): 17,009kg (37,500lbs)

Dimensions: Length 15.01m (49ft 3.5in); Wingspan 9.995m (32ft 9.5in); Height 5.09m (16ft 8.5in)

Powerplant: One Pratt & Whitney F100-PW-220 turbofan

Maximum speed: Mach 2.05 at 1300m (40,000ft)

Range: 3862km (2400 miles)

Ceiling: 16,764m (55,000ft)

Crew: 1

Armament: One M61A1 20mm (0.787in) cannon (500 rd); six hardpoints: AIM-9 Sidewinder, AIM-7 Sparrow, AIM-120 AM-RAAM air-to-air missiles

Block 15

More significant changes were introduced on the next batch of production aircraft: Block 15. These F-16A/Bs were fitted with a larger horizontal stabilizer resulting in a reduction in rotation angle for take-off and permitting flight at higher angles of attack. Other visual identifiers of the Block 15 aircraft included parallel RWR antennas below the radomes and the absence of the blade antenna, which was deleted. In terms of avionics, the Block 15 aircraft had changes made to their AN/APG-66 radar, which now provided a limited track-while-scan capability.

The layout of the cockpit was subject to changes, too, and a Have Quick UHF secure voice radio system was introduced. Certain operators made other changes to their Block 15 aircraft, including the Netherlands, which adapted some of its aircraft to carry the Oude Delft Orpheus reconnaissance pod under the unofficial designation F-16A(R).

The Orpheus pod had previously been used by Dutch RF-104 Starfighters and offered a day/night capability.

An Operational Capability Upgrade (OCU) was also carried out on the Block 15 aircraft, with these F-16A/Bs receiving structural reinforcements along with an enlarged head-up display (HUD) taken from the more advanced F-16C/D. As well as other minor changes, the OCU brought updates to the radar and software, the fire control system and the stores management computer. These changes made the aircraft compatible with AN/ALQ-131 jamming pods. Modifications were also introduced that made it possible to install the more reliable F100-PW-220E engine, providing 118.32kN (26,660lb) of thrust.

MLU Programme

The OCU process for the Block 15 was only a stepping stone towards a much more comprehensive package of

F-16A BLOCK 15B ADF
This General Dynamics F-16A Block 15B ADF, MM.7238 (serial number 80-0615) served with the 5 Stormo of the Italian Air Force.

F-16B BLOCK 20 MLU
Built in the Belgian SABCA (Sociétés Anonyme Belge de
Constructions Aéronautiques) factory, this F-16B Block 20
MLU, serial number ET-612 80-3612, is part of the Royal
Danish Air Force, Eskadrille 727. Esk 727 was the first
Danish squadron to receive the F-16 fighter.

F-16B Block 20 MLU

**Weight (maximum take-
off):** 17,010kg (37,500lbs)
empty, 11467.27kg
(25,281lbs) combat,
17,009.71kg (37,500lbs)
maximum takeoff
Dimensions: Length
15.14m (49ft 8in);
Wingspan 9.97m (32ft 8in);
Height 4.9m (16ft 1in)
Powerplant: One Pratt
& Whitney F100-PW-220
turbofan
Maximum speed:
1472.55km/h (915mph)
at sea level
Range: 1166.77km
(725 miles)
Ceiling: 6598.92m (21,650ft)
Crew: 2
Armament: One M61A1
20mm (0.787in) cannon (500
rd); six hardpoints: AIM-9
Sidewinder, AIM-7 Sparrow,
AIM-120 AMRAAM air-to-air
missiles; AGM-65 Maverick
missile, GBU-31 (JDAM)
2000lb guided bomb,
GBU-38 (JDAM) 500lb
guided bomb

improvements for the F-16A/B
manifested under the Mid-Life
Update (MLU) programme. These
aircraft underwent a thorough
refurbishment and also received
a more modern cockpit derived
from that found in what was,
at the time, the latest F-16C/D
Block 50/52 aircraft. The radar
for the MLU aircraft was the AN/
APG-66(V)2, installed as part of
a modernized suite of avionics
that also included a Global
Positioning System (GPS) for
precise navigation, wide-angle
HUD and a digital terrain mapping
system. The previous three separate
mission computers were replaced
by a single, modular unit. Other
options included a helmet-
mounted sight and a Hazeltine
AN/APX-111 Identification
Friend or Foe (IFF) transponder.
Finally, the cockpit was also made
compatible with night-vision
goggles (NVGs), marking a
significant improvement in night/
adverse-weather capabilities.

The MLU programme saw
four F-16s arrive at Fort Worth in

September 1992 to serve as
the prototypes for the conversion.
Modifications were then
incorporated in existing Block
15 aircraft at different facilities
around the world in what was a
remarkably successful effort. Today,
MLU-standard F-16A/Bs remain
the backbone of a number of
NATO air forces, while others have
been transferred to non-NATO
customers. Bringing essentially the
same level of capability as found
in the more modern F-16C/D
Block 50/52, the MLU aircraft have
provided a very suitable bridging
solution for air forces awaiting the
delivery of the fifth-generation
F-35 Lightning II Joint Strike
Fighter, in particular.

Block 20
The Block 20 aircraft were
produced by General Dynamics
for Taiwan, with the non-standard
number (not ending in a 5) being
selected retrospectively for this
particular customer. The F-16A/
Bs produced for the Republic of
China Air Force (ROCAF) featured

a number of important differences, including the improved AN/APG-66(V)2 radar as found in the MLU aircraft. A specific IFF was fitted for Taiwanese requirements, and the ROCAF aircraft are also compatible with the Raytheon AN/ALQ-183 electronic countermeasures pod, used in preference to the AN/ALQ-131.

F-16 ADF
(Air Defense Fighter)
In October 1986, the US Air Force announced that it was to convert a total of 270 F-16A/B aircraft from the Block 15 production batch to a new standard, known as Air Defense Fighter (ADF), specifically to equip Air National Guard (ANG) units tasked with the defence of the continental United States, under North American Aerospace Defense Command (NORAD). Eventually, the number of ADF conversions was reduced to 241, comprising 217 single-seat F-16As and 24 two-seat F-16Bs. These were intended to serve with 14 ANG (Air National Guard) squadrons.

The ADF specification involved several important changes that would turn the basic F-16 into a much more capable interceptor able to engage bomber and cruise missile targets approaching North America and ensure their detection and destruction at longer ranges. Not only was the long-range interception mission new for the F-16, but the aircraft also lacked a radar-guided air-to-air missile (AAM) suitable for beyond-visual-range engagements.

At the centre of the ADF conversion, therefore, were changes to the AN/APG-66 radar that improved its ability to detect small targets (in the case of cruise missiles) and then also provide the continuous-wave illumination necessary to guide a radar-guided AIM-7 missile to its target. The first launch of an AIM-7 from an F-16 ADF took place in February 1989. Other changes embodied in the F-16 ADF included more advanced IFF (the Teledyne/E-Systems Mk XII), enhanced Electronic Counter-countermeasures (ECCM), provision for Navstar GPS and a datalink that could be used with the AIM-120 Advanced Medium-Range Air-to-Air Missile (AMRAAM). For critical long-range communications, the aircraft received a single side-band high-frequency radio – the Bendix/King ARC-200 – although this was not added to the two-seater version.

Finally, an identification light, producing 150,000 candlepower, was installed in the forward fuselage on the left-hand side. This light helped identify aircraft – typically long-range Soviet bombers – intercepted at night.

Identification of the F-16 ADF could be best achieved by reference to the night identification light on the side of the nose and the IFF antennas ahead of the windshield and below the engine air intake. At the same time, the rudder servo actuators were relocated, resulting in a different position for their associated fairings.

The armament of the F-16 ADF comprised up to six AAMs, with a combination of AIM-9 Sidewinders (for within-visual-range engagements) and medium-range AIM-7 Sparrows. The standard 20mm (0.79in) M61 cannon was also retained.

A-16 FOR CLOSE AIR SUPPORT

A total of 24 US Air Force F-16A/Bs from the Block 10 production batch were selected for modifications for the ground-attack role. Most significantly, the Pave Claw programme added a General Electric GPU-5/A gun pod on the centreline, this store weighing 154kg (339lb). The GPU-5/A pod was fitted with a GAU-13/A cannon, essentially a four-barrel version of the seven-barrel GAU-8/A Avenger as used in the A-10 Thunderbolt II 'tank-buster'. Integration of the gun pod on the F-16 was never completely successful and the aircraft were eventually put into storage.

F-16A Block 15B ADF

Weight: 17,010kg (37,500lbs) empty, 11467.27kg (25,281lb) combat, 17009.71kg (37,500lbs) maximum takeoff

Dimensions: Length 15.01m (49ft 3.5in); Wingspan 9.995m (32ft 9.5in); Height 5.09m (16ft 8.5in)

Powerplant: One Pratt & Whitney F100-PW-220 turbofan

Maximum speed: Mach 2.05 at 40,000ft

Range: 3862km (2400 miles)

Ceiling: 16,764m (55,000ft)

Crew: 1

Armament: One M61A1 20mm (0.787in) cannon; six hardpoints: AIM-9 Sidewinder, AIM-7 Sparrow, AIM-120 AMRAAM air-to-air missiles

Opposite: F-16 ADF
This F-16A ADF served with the 178th Fighter Squadron as part of the 119th Fighter Group, North Dakota Air National Guard (ANG). Built as an F-16A-15K-CF, this Fighting Falcon was delivered to the 388th TFW at Hill AFB, Utah, on 28 July 1983. When the 388th TFW converted to F-16Cs, 82-0926 was earmarked to be upgraded to the ADF configuration by the OALC. After being modified, it went to the 178th FS on 29 March 1990.

Typically, a pair of AIM-7F/M missiles were carried on stations 3 and 7 with AIM-9s on the wingtips. Although there was provision for carriage of the AMRAAM, these missiles were ultimately never delivered to the Air National Guard units flying the F-16 ADF.

The process of converting F-16A/Bs jets to ADF standard was undertaken at the US Air Force's Ogden Air Logistics Center (OALC) at Hill Air Force Base, Utah. General Dynamics provided the conversion kits, and the last of the ADF jets completed the conversion process in early 1992.

Before the F-16 ADF commenced frontline service on behalf of NORAD, the aircraft was subject to a developmental test at Edwards Air Force Base, California. Subsequently, an operational test and evaluation work was carried out by the 57th

RF-16 RECCE PROPOSAL

From early on in its career, the F-16 was used for reconnaissance missions, with various different podded sensors, something that was pioneered by the Royal Netherlands Air Force (RNLAF) as it sought to field a replacement for the RF-104G Starfighter. These aircraft were initially modified to carry the Orpheus reconnaissance pod.

At the same time, however, General Dynamics was looking at offering customers a tailor-made reconnaissance version of the Fighting Falcon, known as the RF-16. This effort was given impetus by the US Air Force, which, as of 1988, was considering replacing its RF-4C Phantom II fleet with RF-16s.

The RF-16 as outlined for the US Air Force would have been fitted with the Control Data Corporation ATARS (Advanced Tactical Air Reconnaissance System) pod, carried on the centreline station.

ATARS was a notably advanced pod for this time, with various sensors including an electro-optical system that allowed imagery to be relayed to a ground station in real time, using a datalink. Eventually the US Air Force changed its plans and abandoned ATARS, although the system was still taken up by the US Navy, which introduced it on its F/A-18 Hornet in an internal, pallet-mounted configuration.

DUTCH F-16A
This F-16A Block 1 Fighting Falcon, J-216, served with 306 Squadron, Royal Netherlands Air Force. The Dutch replaced their F-104G Starfighters equipped with a reconnaissance system developed by the Oudedelft company with F-16 Fighting Falcons.

Fighter Weapons Wing at Nellis Air Force Base, Nevada.

Air National Guard Operators

The first frontline operator of the F-16 ADF was the Oregon ANG, specifically the 114th Fighter Squadron, based at Kingsley Field in Klamath Falls. This unit provided training to ANG pilots that would fly the F-16 ADF within operational units, which ultimately comprised the following squadrons:

111th Fighter Squadron Texas ANG

119th Fighter Squadron New Jersey ANG

134th Fighter Squadron Vermont ANG

136th Fighter Squadron New York ANG

159th Fighter Squadron Florida ANG

169th Fighter Squadron Illinois ANG*

171st Fighter Squadron Missouri ANG

178th Fighter Squadron North Dakota ANG

179th Fighter Squadron Minnesota ANG

186th Fighter Squadron Montana ANG

194th Fighter Squadron California ANG

F-16B *Netz*

Weight (empty):
7386.75kg (16,285lbs)

Dimensions: Length
15.14m (49ft 8in); Wingspan
9.97m (32ft 8in); Height
4.9m (16ft 1in)

Powerplant: One Pratt
& Whitney F100-PW-220
turbofan

Maximum speed:
1690km/h (1050mph)

Range: 1166.77km
(725 miles)

Ceiling: 6598.92m (21,650ft)

Crew: 2

Armament: One M61A1
20mm (0.787in) cannon
(500 rd); six hardpoints:
AIM-9 Sidewinder, Python
3 missiles; ground attack:
AGM-65 Maverick missile,
70mm unguided rockets, Tal
2 cluster bomb, Mk82 500lb
bomb, Mk84 2000lb bomb

198th Fighter Squadron
Puerto Rico ANG*
* not assigned to NORAD.

The availability of the Fighting Falcon, in general, made the F-16 ADF a suitable candidate for the ADF mission, and it was a more than capable successor to the F-4 Phantoms and F-106 Delta Darts that most of these units previously operated.

However, the fact is that the aircraft arrived just as the Soviet Union was crumbling and just as the significance of the aerial threat posed to North America was being entirely reconsidered. The demise of the Soviet Union led to wide-ranging defence cutbacks across the US military, and the Air Force was no exception. In particular, the ADF units were subject to these cuts, with a total

GENERAL DYNAMICS F-16B
FIGHTING FALCON
In Israeli service, the early F-16As and F-16Bs were known as *Netz* (Hawk). F-16B 004 was one of the first aircraft to be delivered from Fort Worth, Texas, in July 1980 and served with the 253 Tayeset, based in Hayl Ha' avir, Ramon. This artwork shows the aircraft on a mission in 1981.

of 11 such squadrons soon being brought down to just three (the 178th, 179th and 186th Fighter Squadrons).

The sudden availability of recently converted F-16 ADF airframes provided a windfall for other air forces, however. Although the threat from the Warsaw Pact had now disappeared, many countries needed to upgrade their fighter fleets, replacing their ageing Cold War-era equipment.

Overseas sales

In this way, second-hand F-16 ADF aircraft were sold to Portugal, which acquired a total of 17 F-16As and three F-16Bs that had been upgraded. These were transferred under the Peace Atlantic programme. The jets were provided together with AIM-7 AAMs, although Portugal soon began operating them in a dual-role capacity, with armament for ground-attack missions. Another customer for second-hand F-16 ADF aircraft emerged in the Middle East, where Jordan acquired 25 examples under the Peace Falcon initiative.

Below: ANG F-16

An F-16 from the Toledo Air National Guard, Ohio, flies near the wing of a KC-135 to position itself for refueling during a sortie in support of Operation Northern Watch (1997–2003), enforcing the no-fly zone over northern Iraq.

Opposite: SPIN CHUTE

A close-up of the spin chute mounted on the rear fuselage of the AFTI F-16, a safety device designed to prevent the loss of aircraft in spin conditions.

F-16 ADVANCED FIGHTER TECHNOLOGY INTEGRATION (AFTI)

To investigate unconventional control of an aircraft in flight, in 1978 the Air Force Systems Command's Flight Dynamics Laboratory backed the modification of the sixth FSD F-16A under the Advanced Fighter Technology Integration (AFTI) programme. After modification, it made its first flight at Fort Worth on 10 July 1982.

Drawing upon the experience of the YF-16 Control Configured Vehicle (CCV), the AFTI F-16 was fitted with the same pair of canted canard fins below the engine air intake. Meanwhile, an enlarged spine accommodated additional electronics. Avionics changes included a full-authority triplex Digital Flight Control System (DFCS) and an Automated Maneuvering Attack System (AMAS).

The AFTI F-16 also incorporated some features that were notably advanced for the time, including a Voice-Controlled Interactive Device (VCID). Initially allowing the pilot to give only one-word commands to the flight control system, the VCID was made progressively more complex; ultimately, it was able to respond to more complex multi-word commands.

The pilot was also provided with a Helmet-Mounted Target Designation Sight, something that is, by now, a familiar feature in advanced fighter cockpits. In the AFTI F-16, the pilot was able to use the helmet sight to designate a target, which could then be locked on, with the forward-looking infrared (FLIR) sensor and radar being automatically slaved to the pilot's head movement.

In total, the AFTI F-16 completed 275 test sorties at Edwards Air Force Base, California. The testing was divided into three phases, respectively: evaluation of the DFCS and demonstration of direct translational manoeuvring; testing of the FLIR sensor in the wing root and the AMAS; and Close Air Support (CAS) studies and testing of the AFTI Advanced or Automatic Ground Collision Avoidance System (Auto-GCAS).

BELGIAN F-16B

A special livery Belgian Air Force F-16B dual-seater fighter taking off from Florennes Air Base, Belgium, June 2017.

F-16C/D: Vipers for a New Era

As we have seen, it didn't take long for General Dynamics' original proposal for an 'austere' day fighter to be superseded by the F-16A/B that added a radar and a degree of multirole capability. However, these first-generation F-16s were still primarily air defence fighters, with a limited capacity to undertake air-to-ground missions and, even then, primarily with unguided armament such as bombs and rockets.

NATO MISSION
Two USAF Europe F-16Cs fly in formation during a mission in support of NATO Operation Allied Force. The F-16s are from the 510th Fighter Squadron 'Buzzards', Aviano Air Base, Italy and are carrying a full air-to-air combat load to include AIM-120 missiles, drop tanks and an electronic jamming pod. The lead F-16 is a single seat F-16CG and has both a laser designating pod as well as a FLIR (Forward Looking Infrared) pod on the intake sides. The second F-16 is a F-16DG and is only capable of carrying the FLIR pod.

First flown on 19 June 1984, the single-seat F-16C was an altogether more capable warplane than the F-16A/B. Together with the two-seat F-16D model, these 'second-generation' Vipers introduced a range of improvements that considerably boosted their combat potential, especially as regards multirole missions.

In terms of identification, the F-16C/D aircraft could be distinguished by an enlarged base for the vertical tail, forming a distinctive 'island' at the bottom of the fin. The additional space this provided was originally intended to accommodate the internal Airborne Self-Protection Jammer (ASPJ), although the US Air Force later abandoned this

plan. Instead, F-16C/Ds continued to fly with external electronic countermeasures pods.

Advanced cockpit

Less visible but important changes introduced in the F-16C/D included a more advanced cockpit with a GEC head-up display (HUD). While the HUD on the earlier F-16A/B featured a keyboard control console to the left, the new HUD placed the console at the base. It was also accompanied by an improved data display, with the most critical information now being presented at eye level. This was intended to better exploit the potential of the Hands-on Throttle and Stick (HOTAS) controls that had been

a Viper feature from the start. The F-16C/D was fielded with an all-new radar, the Westinghouse AN/APG-68 multimode system replacing the previous AN/APG-66. The new radar provided increased range, enhanced resolution and a wider selection of operating modes. Importantly, the new radar was also compatible with more capable weapons, including the latest AIM-120 Advanced

ORIENTATION FLIGHT
Captain Steve Strandburg, from the Alabama Air National Guard (ANG) prepares to fly Lt. Gen. Serhiy Onyschenko in an Air National Guard F-16D for an orientation flight at Mirgorod Air Base, Ukraine, during Safe Skies 2011.

ACAT TECHNOLOGY
A US Air Force F-16D Automatic
Collision Avoidance Technology
(ACAT) aircraft takes off from Edwards
Air Force Base on a flight originating
from NASA's Dryden Flight Research
Centre. Dryden and the Air Force
Research Laboratory are collaborating
to develop collision avoidance
technologies that would reduce the risk
of ground and mid-air collisions.

Medium-Range Air-to-Air Missile
(AMRAAM) for beyond-visual-
range aerial engagements and the
AGM-65D Maverick with imaging
infrared guidance for air-to-ground
missions. Other general armament
options remained broadly similar,
including the M61A1 Vulcan
cannon with 511 rounds and
external stores of up to 7575kg
(16,700lb).

**Multi-Stage Improvement
Program (MSIP)**
While these changes were included
in the F-16C/D from the start, the
aircraft also added progressive
new modifications as production
progressed. As well as receiving

new equipment on the production
line, earlier aircraft were also
subject to enhancements embodied
in the Multi-Stage Improvement
Program (MSIP), which addressed
avionic and airframe changes. It
was followed by MSIP II, which
introduced further changes.
Together, these two efforts
made the F-16C/D better able
to fly and fight at night and in
adverse weather. Later aircraft
also introduced a gold-tinted
cockpit canopy to improve radar
reflectivity.

The first production batch
of F-16C/D aircraft was covered
by Block 25, with manufacture
beginning in July 1984. This block

F-16N

The F-16N was developed for the US Navy as an aggressor aircraft to replace the ageing F4 and F5 fighters used to simulate hostiles. It carries specialist instrumentation to enable engagements to be monitored during – and studied after – the mission. There was no intention to create a fully navalized F-16; the F-16N never received the strengthened undercarriage necessary for carrier operations. A total of 22 single-seat and 4 two-seat F-16Ns served from 1988 to 1998 but were withdrawn from flight operations after cracks were discovered in their structural components.

NAVY FLIERS
A US Navy F-16N Block 30C,
from VF-126, circa 1993.

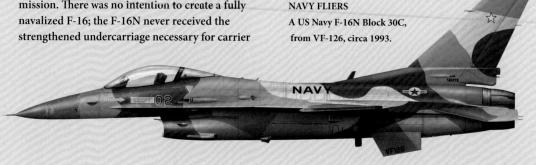

TOP GUN
Two US Navy/US Marine Corps General Dynamics F-16N Viper and two Douglas A-4F Skyhawk of the United States Navy Fighter Weapons School ('Top Gun') flying over Lower Otay Reservoir, Chula Vista, California, 1991.

NF-16D BLOCK 30
NF-16D Variable In-flight Simulator Aircraft (VISTA). Operated by the US Air
Force Test Pilot School at Edwards Air Force Base, it was redesignated as the
X-62A in June 2021. The NF-16 VISTA started life as a F-16D Block 30, which
later received numerous upgrades and modifications.

F-16C BLOCK 32
A USAF General Dynamics F-16C
Block 32D, serial number 86-0291,
AFRES, 302nd Fighter Squadron
(302 FS), circa 2016.

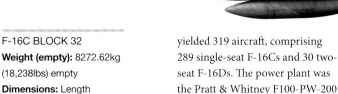

F-16C BLOCK 32
Weight (empty): 8272.62kg
(18,238lbs) empty
Dimensions: Length
15.04m (49ft 4in); Wingspan
9.4488m (31ftin); Height
5.09m (16ft 8.5in)
Powerplant: One Pratt
& Whitney F100-PW-220
turbofan or General Electric
F110-GE-100 turbofan
Maximum speed: Mach
2.02 at 40,000ft
Range: 579km (360 miles)
Ceiling: 55,000ft (16,764m)
Crew: 1
Armament: One 20mm
(0.787in) M61A1 six-barrel
rotary cannon, plus six
hardpoints

yielded 319 aircraft, comprising
289 single-seat F-16Cs and 30 two-
seat F-16Ds. The power plant was
the Pratt & Whitney F100-PW-200
turbofan engine.

Block 30/32
With the Block 30/32 production
batches, General Dynamics ¬– for
the first time – introduced options
for either the F100 (Block 32)
or the General Electric F110-
GE-100 turbofan (Block 30),
thanks to a reconfigured engine
bay. This effort was known as the
Alternative Fighter Engine (AFE)
programme. While the F100
produced 106.05kN (28,840lb), the
F110 delivered 128.9kN (28,984lb)
of thrust.

With the more powerful F110
engine from General Electric,
changes had to be made to the
F-16's engine intake to provide
for the required increase in
airflow. The early Block 30 aircraft
(including the F-16Ns that were
produced for the US Navy)
retained the original air intake,
however, although this soon
gave way to a larger intake when
the width of these aircraft were
increased by roughly 0.3m (1ft),
leading them to be colloquially
known as 'Big Mouths'. Meanwhile,
all the standard Block 32 aircraft
with the Pratt & Whitney power
plant retained the original intake,
formally described as the 'normal
shock inlet'.

SAFETY CHECKS
US Air Force Senior Airman Tyler
Spohn, crew chief with the New Jersey
Air National Guard's 177th Fighter
Wing, performs final safety checks under
the wing of an F-16D Fighting Falcon
as he preps the jet for launch during
Operation Snowbird at Davis-Monthan
Air Force Base, Arizona, 2014.

F-16C BLOCK 40G
A USAF General Dynamics F-16CG
Night Falcon, Block 40G, serial number
89-2136, from the 51st Fighter Wing
(51 FW), circa 2021.

F-16C BLOCK 40G
Weight (empty): 8272.62kg
(18,238lbs)
Dimensions: Length
15.04m (49ft 4in); Wingspan
9.4488m (31ft 3in); Height
5.09m (16ft 8.5in)
Powerplant: One General
Electric F110-GE-100
turbofan
Maximum Speed: Mach
2.02 at 40,000ft
Range: Maximum ferry
range with external fuel:
3862km (2400 miles)
Ceiling: 16,764m (55,000ft)
Crew: 1
Armament: One M61A1
20mm (0.787in) cannon;
six hardpoints: AIM-9
Sidewinder, AIM-7 Sparrow,
AIM-120 AMRAAM air-to-
air missiles; ground attack:
AGM-65 Maverick missile,
GBU-31 (JDAM) 2000lb
guided bomb; anti-radiation:
AGM-45 Shrike, AGM-88
HARM missiles; maritime
strike: AGM-84 Harpoon
missile

The Block 30/32 provided some important new armament options as well, with compatibility for the AGM-45 Shrike and AGM-88 High-speed Anti-Radiation Missile (HARM), both used to target enemy ground-based radar emitters as part of the defence suppression mission, known within the US Air Force as the 'Wild Weasel' mission.

Ultimately, a total of 501 of the Block 30/32 aircraft rolled out of the factory, with the breakdown being 446 single-seat F-16Cs and 55 two-seat F-16Ds.

The Block 30/32 aircraft represented a considerable advance over the Block 25 jets, let alone the F-16A/B, but General Dynamics was not done with its successive Viper improvements.

Block 40/42
The next F-16C/D production batch comprised Block 40/42 aircraft. Here, as in the previous batch, the Block 40 aircraft were powered by the F110 engine, while the Block 42 aircraft were fitted with the F100.

Perhaps the most significant advance incorporated in the F-16C/D Block 40/42 aircraft was a much-improved night and adverse-weather capability, leading to these jets sometimes being unofficially referred to as 'Night Falcons'.

The Block 40/42 aircraft were compatible with the Low-Altitude Navigation and Targeting Infrared for Night (LANTIRN) system, consisting of a pair of pods mounted externally beneath the aircraft. The targeting pod contained: a high-resolution, forward-looking infrared (FLIR) sensor, providing the pilot with an infrared image of the target; a laser designator and rangefinder for precise delivery of laser-guided munitions; a missile boresight correlator for automatic lock-on of AGM-65D missiles; and software for automatic target tracking.

Meanwhile, the navigation pod contained a terrain-following radar and a fixed infrared sensor, providing visual cues and inputs to the F-16's flight control system. This allowed the jet to maintain

LOW-OBSERVABLE ASYMMETRIC NOZZLE (LOAN)

Low-observable ('stealth') technologies are usually aimed at reducing either an aircraft's radar return or its thermal signature. By far the hottest and most obvious part of an aircraft is the exhaust from its jet engine; reducing thermal signature not only helps conceal the aircraft but may also diminish the effectiveness of thermal-homing- (infrared-) guided weapons or make flare decoys more effective. A lower-signature aircraft may be a less attractive target or might be effectively hidden by hotter and brighter flares between its exhaust and the infrared seeker of a missile.

A hot exhaust is an inevitable consequence of jet propulsion, so reducing thermal signature requires either giving the gases a chance to cool somewhat before being exhausted or concealing them in some manner. In some aircraft, such as the A-10, exhausts are positioned so that the tail section obscures them from the most likely angle of attack with a thermal-guided weapon.

This is simply not possible with the F-16, and with only so much room aboard the aircraft, it was not possible to create much natural cooling distance. Fortunately, a suitable technology was already under development.

The Low-Observable Asymmetric Nozzle (LOAN) was developed in the 1990s for the Joint Strike Fighter (JSF) programme. In 1996, it was evaluated for use in place of the F-16's standard exhaust. By a combination of shaping, materials and an advanced cooling system, the LOAN was found to significantly reduce thermal signature and radar return. The lower-temperature exhaust also placed less strain on the nozzle divergent flaps, increasing their life and thereby reducing maintenance overhead.

LOAN was not adopted for use aboard new-build F-16s, though experience was gained which would prove useful in the JSF/F-35 project. It is possible that future variants of the F-16 may introduce this technology to create a relatively low-cost alternative to high-end 'stealth' fighters. This would reflect a return to the origins of the F-16 as a low-cost, highly effective combat aircraft.

F-16C BLOCK 42
This flamboyantly marked Block 42 F-16C wears the colours of the 125th Fighter
Squadron, a unit of the Oklahoma Air National Guard that is assigned to the
138th Fighter Wing located at Tulsa Air National Guard Base, Oklahoma.
Since the early 1990s the unit has made frequent combat deployments to the
Middle East, taking part in Operations Northern Watch, Southern Watch, Iraqi
Freedom and New Dawn.

ISRAELI F-16I *SUFA*

First flown in late 2003, the F-16I was developed for the Israeli air force from the F-16D Block 50/52. It is known as Soufa, or Storm, in Israeli service. Adopting the two-seat model gave the Israeli air force trainers as well as combat aircraft, with any given aircraft able to operate as either. This was a significant investment, with deliveries from 2004 to 2009 ultimately resulting in a force of 362 aircraft.

SMALL COMBAT RADIUS

One concern about the F-16, particularly in its early versions, was its relatively small combat radius without external fuel tanks. Adding tanks to the inboard 'wet' pylons increased range at the price of reduced performance and weapons load. This was tackled by fitting low-drag conformal fuel tanks on the sides of the fuselage. The impact on the aircraft's flight characteristics was minimal, allowing these hardpoints to be used for additional weaponry.

The F-16I uses advanced navigation and terrain-following systems to increase survivability by flying very low in ground attack mode. It can deliver precision-guided munitions, but even unguided weapons are greatly enhanced by technological aiming assistance, especially when launched from very low altitude.

F-16I *SUFA* (STORM)

This Israeli Air Force Lockheed Martin F-16D, Block 52, serial number 00-1035, dates from 2005. The two-seat F-16I is one of the most important long-range strike assets available to the Israeli Air Force. A total of 102 of these jets were supplied to Israel, where the first examples began to arrive in 2004, while the final examples were handed over in 2009. The aircraft serve with four frontline squadrons and have seen considerable combat action, including raids on Syria.

F-16I SUFA (STORM)

Weight (maximum take-off): 23,582kg (51,989lb)	**Ceiling:** 18,288m (60,000ft)
Dimensions: Length 15.03m (49ft 4in), Wingspan 9.45m (31ft 0in), Height 5.09m (16ft 7in)	**Crew:** 2
Powerplant: One Pratt & Whitney F100-PW-229 turbofan rated at 131.5kN (29,560lb) with afterburning	**Armament:** One 20mm (0.787in) M61A1 six-barrel rotary cannon; plus up to 7700kg (17,000lb) of disposable stores carried on six underwing, two wingtip and one centreline hardpoint (including Rafael's Python 5 infrared-guided air-to-air missile)
Maximum speed: Mach 2.05	
Range: 4217km (2620 miles), ferry with drop tanks	

F-16C BLOCK 52

Weight (maximum take-off): 19,187kg (42,300lb)

Dimensions: Length 15.06m (49ft 5in), Wingspan 9.96m (32ft 8in), Height 4.9m (16ft)

Powerplant: One General Electric F110-GE-129 turbofan rated at 131kN (29,500lb) thrust with afterburning; (Block 52) one Pratt & Whitney F100-PW-229 turbofan rated at 131.5kN (29,560lb) with afterburning

Maximum speed: Mach 2.05

Range: 4217km (2620 miles), with drop tanks

Ceiling: 18,288m (60,000ft)

Crew: 1

Armament: One 20mm (0.787in) M61A1 six-barrel rotary cannon, plus up to 7700kg (17,000lb) of disposable stores carried on six underwing, two wingtip and one centreline hardpoint

a pre-selected altitude above the terrain and avoid obstacles. The infrared image from the pod is also displayed to the pilot, via the HUD.

Block 50/52

The next major iteration of the F-16C/D was the Block 50/52 aircraft. The first single-seat F-16C from this block took its maiden flight on 22 October 1991. The Block 50/52 aircraft introduced a more advanced radar, the AN/APG-68(V)5, which was coupled to an improved avionics computer. Other avionics changes included a Have Quick IIA radio, a Have Sync anti-jam VHF radio, a wide-angle HUD and full HARM integration. The Block 50/52 aircraft also benefitted from enhancements to their self-protection suites, with a new Tracor AN/ALE-47 chaff/flare dispenser and An/ALR-56M Radar Warning Receiver (RWR).

Like the Block 30/32 and Block 40/42 aircraft that came before them, the Block 50/52 jets were beneficiaries of the Alternative Fighter Engine (AFE) programme, although now the different power plants were also available in uprated form. The Improved Performance Engine (IPE) versions of the Pratt & Whitney and General Electric turbofans were the F100-PW-229 and the F110-GE-129, respectively producing 129.4kN (29,100lb) and 131.6kN (29,588lb) of thrust.

However, the IPE initiative did not proceed entirely smoothly, with problems being experienced with the Block 52 version during the developmental test phase in the summer of 1991. This meant that some of these aircraft were refitted with older versions of the F100, pending a redesign of the fourth fan stage of the F100-PW-229 engine.

F-16C BLOCK 52

A Polish Air Force Lockheed Martin F-16C Block 52 Fighting Falcon, 4055, serial number 03-0055, circa 2014.

General Dynamics began to deliver the first of the Block 50/52 aircraft to the US Air Force in December 1991, with the initial operator being the 388th Fighter Wing at Luke Air Force Base, Arizona, for training.

The first of the frontline units to receive these aircraft was the 52nd Fighter Wing, assigned to US Air Forces in Europe and based at Spangdahlem Air Base in Germany.

Wild Weasel mission
The US Air Force required a portion of its Block 50/52 to undertake the full spectrum of the Wild Weasel mission – a United States Air Force code name for an aircraft equipped with anti-radiation missiles designed to suppress enemy air defences. This superseded the F-4G that was previously used in this role (latterly alongside earlier F-16 variants). With the Block 50/52D standard,

the aircraft was provided with the HARM Targeting System (HTS), including the AN/ASQ-213 pod carried under the starboard side of the engine intake.

Outside of the United States, there have also been more radical developments of the F-16C/D, most dramatically the 'big spine' modifications applied to Israel's Block 30 and Block 40 aircraft and also adopted by other international operators.

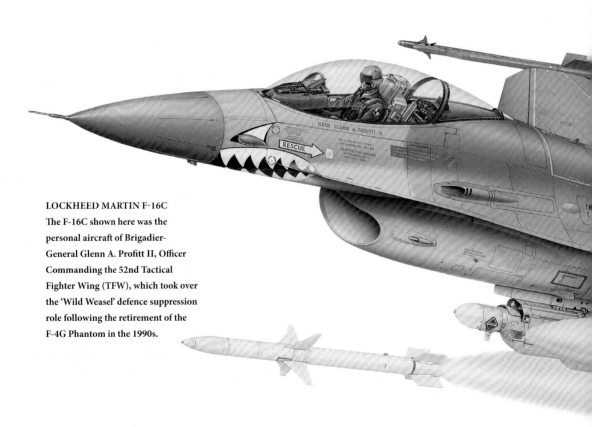

LOCKHEED MARTIN F-16C
The F-16C shown here was the personal aircraft of Brigadier-General Glenn A. Profitt II, Officer Commanding the 52nd Tactical Fighter Wing (TFW), which took over the 'Wild Weasel' defence suppression role following the retirement of the F-4G Phantom in the 1990s.

LOCKHEED MARTIN F-16C

Weight (empty): 8936kg (19,700lbs)

Dimensions: Length 15.08m (49ft 5in); Wingspan 9.8m (32ft 8in); Height 5.09m (16ft 8.5in)

Powerplant: One Pratt and Whitney F100-PW-200/220/229 or General Electric F110-GE-100/129

Maximum Speed: Mach 2.02 at 40,000ft

Range: Maximum ferry range with external fuel: 3700km (2300 miles)

Ceiling: 16,764m (55,000ft)

Crew: 1

Armament: One M61A1 20mm (0.787in) cannon; six hardpoints: AIM-9 Sidewinder, AIM-7 Sparrow, AIM-120 AMRAAM air-to-air missiles; ground attack: AGM-65 Maverick missile, GBU-31 (JDAM) 2000lb guided bomb; anti-radiation: AGM-45 Shrike, AGM-88 HARM missiles; maritime strike: AGM-84 Harpoon missile

F-16ES

The F-16ES (Enhanced Strategic) was developed to give the F-16 increased range and flexibility. This move was part of a general evolution away from the relatively cheap and simple light fighter originally conceived. Development of this sort is all but inevitable in any aircraft that lasts more than a few years in service. Users will always want more from even the most successful design, and it is

F-16CJ
Captain Jeff "Tuck" Cohen from the
55th Fighter Squadron, 20th Fighter
Wing, Shaw Air Force Base, South
Carolina, fires an AIM-120C Advanced
Medium Range Air-to-Air Missile
(AMRAAM) from his F-16CJ fighter
at a BQM-34 sub-scale drone.

generally more cost-effective to
evolve an existing aircraft than
it is to develop an entirely new
one. There are limits to this, of
course, but the F-16 has not yet
approached them.

The catalyst for this new
version was an Israeli requirement
for a new strike fighter. To fit this
requirement, the F-16 was given
large conformal fuel tanks along
the sides of the fuselage. With
external tanks also carried, the
F-16ES can deliver two Mk84
bombs or their guided variants

out to a range of just over 1,000
miles whilst retaining some air-
to-air capability. Although this
performance is impressive and
comparable to the F-15E Strike
Eagle, the latter was ultimately
chosen by the IAF.

Both aircraft approached the
high-capability strike fighter
mission from entirely different
directions. The F-15 started out
as a pure air-to-air platform with
the mantra 'not a pound for air
to ground', whereas the F-16 was
always intended for low-level
strike operations. The F-16 grew in
complexity and capability from a
relatively humble beginning, whilst
the F-15 started out as a top-end
performer but had to be adapted
for an entirely different role.

Other features implemented
on the F-16ES included the
internalization of the Forward-

Looking Infrared (FLIR) system
previously carried in an external
pod as part of the Low Altitude
Navigation Targeting Infrared for
Night (LANTIRN) system.

Moving the system inside
the aircraft eliminated drag
associated with the pod, and the
effect of the FLIR mountings was
found to be minimal.

Continued Development
The end result of these upgrades
was a more capable F-16 made
so without compromising its
excellent agility – though naturally,
there were cost increases. The
F-16ES project ultimately led to
the F-16E/F Block 60 variant.
This aircraft is a milestone in
the development of the F-16,
sufficiently different to preceding
versions that it was redesignated
from a C/D variant to E/F. It was

planned that F-16E/F would enter service with the United States Air Force, but efforts were instead directed towards the fifth-generation F-35. Development continued with the United Arab Emirates as the target market, creating what is sometimes called the Desert Falcon. In addition to greater fuel capacity and therefore range, further internalization of electronics was undertaken. Systems that had gradually been added as pods were moved to a new dorsal compartment between the cockpit and the tail, creating the 'big spine' characteristic of these variants.

What had been add-ons to the earlier models were now integrated into the redesigned model, taking the Enhanced Strategic concept far beyond what had originally been envisaged.

QF-16

The QF-16 programme is the latest in a line of remote-controlled target plane projects. Obsolete aircraft, or examples with defects requiring removal from active service, are converted into target drones for training. Previous designs used include the F-4 Phantom, designated QF-4, and the F-106 Delta Dart. Target aircraft are naturally expended, so as the numbers of QF-4s available dwindled a replacement had to be sourced. Targets would have to be capable of posing a significant challenge to a modern fighter and also be available in sufficient quantity. The F-16 was an obvious choice.

The contract for conversion of a test batch was awarded to Boeing in 2010, with six examples converted for evaluation. These included Block 15, Block 25 and Block 30 aircraft. Conversion involved removing non-essential systems and installing a flight termination device for use in the event of control loss. This is essentially an

QF-16
A QF-16C Block 30, #85-1455 (QF-11), from the 82nd Aerial Targets Squadron (ATRS) of the US Air Force, based at Tyndall Air Force Base, Florida.

explosive device capable of disabling the aircraft sufficiently that it will crash. Manual controls are left in place to allow drones to be flown from the cockpit, with a remote-control system added during conversion along with instrumentation to evaluate the performance of weapons used against the drone.

The initial piloted flight was recorded in May 2012, and the first remote-controlled flight was achieved in September 2013. QF-16s can conduct electronic warfare and are equivalent in performance to a piloted F-16, including unmanned supersonic flight. The current operator is 82nd Aerial Targets Squadron (ATARS), based at Tyndall AFB.

MITSUBISHI F-2

In 1960, the Japan Air Self-Defense Force (JASDF) was equipped with aircraft bought overseas but sought to create an indigenous trainer for its pilots. In 1967, a contract was awarded to Mitsubishi Heavy Industries for what became the T-2. This was later developed into a single-seat strike fighter designated F-1, which first flew in 1975 and entered service in 1978. As is often the case, the F-1 had not been long in service before its replacement began to be considered.

Development of what would become the F-2 by Mitsubishi Heavy Industries began in 1988 with a Memorandum of Understanding between the USA and Japan. Flight was recorded in 1997, and production began in 1998. The first examples were delivered to the Air Self-Defense Force in 2005. Like other F-16 models, the F-2 is produced in single-seat and dual-seat configurations, as F-2A and F-2B respectively.

The aircraft is a collaboration between US and Japanese companies, with engines supplied by General Electric and avionics by Lockheed Martin. Other electronic systems are Japanese or international collaborations, whilst most structural components are produced by Japanese firms including Fuji and Kawasaki. Part of the fuselage and the wings are manufactured by Mitsubishi, which uses a co-cured honeycomb structure rather than the more conventional post-cured version. The F-2 is the first fighter aircraft to use this method.

Gun armament is conventional, mounting the same M61A1 0.79in (20mm) rotary cannon used in other F-16 variants. External stores are carried on thirteen hardpoints. The wingtip pylons can mount small air-to-air missiles, and there is a large centreline pylon capable of carrying an external fuel tank. Five pylons under each wing use common rail launchers to permit a variety of weapons to be carried. These include Sidewinder and Sparrow missiles along with the Japanese AAM-3 air-to-air missile. The inner pylons on each wing are 'wet' and can carry fuel tanks if required. In a ground attack mission, the F-2 can make use of cluster or conventional bombs or unguided rockets. Japan's strategic situation makes maritime strikes a necessity, and to this end, the F-2 can launch Type-80 missiles. These weapons can also be deployed by other Japanese combat aircraft and are capable of striking land targets in addition to ships.

F-2A

This single-seat F-2A, serial number 03-8509, wears the samurai insignia of the Japan Air Self-Defense Force's 3 Hikotai on the tail. After two XF-2A prototypes had been completed, the JASDF received 62 production F-2As, the last of these being delivered in September 2011.

MITSUBISHI F-2B

Weight (maximum take-off): 22,100kg (48,722lb)

Dimensions: Length 15.5m (50ft 8in); Wingspan 11.1m (36ft 5in); Height 5m (16ft 4in)

Powerplant: One General Electric F110-GE-100/129 Turbofan

Maximum speed: Mach 2

Range: 833km (518 miles)

Ceiling: 58,727ft (17,900m)

Crew: 2

Armament: One 20mm (0.787in) JM61A1 six-barrel rotary cannon, plus maximum weapon load of 8085kg (17,824lb)

F-2B

Mainly employed for training, the two-seat F-2Bs, such as serial number 33-8122, are mainly assigned to 21 Hikotai, part of the JASDF's Air Training Command, and based at Matsushima. The F-2B production run encompassed two XF-2B prototypes and 32 production examples.

MITSUBISHI F-2A

Weight (maximum take-off): 22,100kg (48,722lb)

Dimensions: Length 15.52m (50ft 11in), Wingspan 11.125m (36ft 6in) including wingtip pylons, Height 16ft (4.9m)

Powerplant: One General Electric F110-IHI-129 turbofan rated at 131kN (29,500lb) thrust with afterburning

Maximum speed: Mach 1.7

Range: 833km (518 miles)

Ceiling: 18,000m (59,000ft)

Crew: 1

Armament: One 20mm (0.787in) JM61A1 six-barrel rotary cannon, plus maximum weapon load of 8085kg (17,824lb)

F-16E/F:
Beyond Block 50

The Block 60 designation for the F-16 was originally reserved for a specialized ground-attack version of the aircraft unofficially known as the F/A-16, which would have followed on from the less than successful A-16 proposal. Among other features, the F/A-16 would have added a 30mm (1.18in) cannon in place of the standard 20mm (0.79in) M61A1.

DESERT FALCON

A United Arab Emirates F-16E Desert Falcon, Block 60, flies over southern Arizona. The 162nd Fighter Wing at Tucson International Airport maintains and operates a squadron of Block 60s for the purpose of training the UAE Air Force in the advanced multirole fighter.

With no US Air Force interest in the F/A-16, the Block 60 designation then re-emerged in the form of several studies aimed at winning orders from the United Arab Emirates (UAE). Perhaps the most radical of these proposals was the F-16U, which featured a stretched fuselage as well as a new tailless delta configuration with a trapezoidal wing.

Ultimately, the UAE opted for the F-16 but in a much more orthodox configuration, although the suite of sensors and weapons turned out to be among the most advanced of any of the Vipers. Essentially an evolutionary step ahead of the previous Block 50/52 aircraft, the Block 60 for the UAE is designated F-16E in single-seat

form and F-16F as the two-seater. Collectively, these aircraft are known as Desert Falcons.

F-16/E/F

The F-16E/F retains the Conformal Fuel Tanks (CFTs) that were introduced as an option on the Block 50/52, providing a significant increase in range without losing valuable external stores carriage below the wings and under the fuselage. The avionics suite of the Desert Falcon includes a Northrop Grumman AN/APG-80 Multi-mode Active Electronically Scanned Array (AESA) agile-beam radar, which is claimed to offer a range of around three times greater that of a US Air Force Block 50 F-16C. Indeed, the AN/APG-80

F-16E
A United Arab Emirates Air Force (UAEAF) Lockheed Martin F-16E, serial number 3078, takes off during the Dubai Air Show, 2007.

is said to have even greater range than the AN/APG-63 radar found on the much larger F-15C. One defining characteristic of the new radar is the removal of the standard pitot probe from the tip of the nose.

The radar is also combined with a new Northrop Grumman AN/ASQ-28 Internal FLIR and Targeting System (IFTS). This is a significant advance over the previous Low-Altitude Navigation and Targeting Infrared for Night

(LANTIRN), which relied on separate navigation and targeting pods, the new system being fully integrated within the airframe. This not only reduces aerodynamic drag but frees up the intake hardpoints for other stores, if required.

Inside the cockpit, the F-16E/F benefits from an all-new configuration with fully digital instruments, the most important being a set of three 12.7cm x 17.78cm (5in x 7in) colour multifunction displays. New avionics also include a secure radio and datalink from Thales.

Desert Falcon

The Desert Falcon is notably well protected against enemy air defence systems, using the Northrop Grumman Falcon Edge integrated electronic countermeasures system. The centrepiece of this is the AN/ALQ-165 Airborne Self-Protection Jammer (ASPJ), originally developed to fulfil US Navy and Air Force requirements.

Another major change brought about by the F-16E/F is an uprated powerplant, the General Electric F110-GE-132 engine producing 144.57kN (32,500lb) of thrust. While the Desert Falcon was the first F-16 production variant to use the new turbofan, it had been previously tested using a modified US Air Force F-16C at the Air Force Flight Test Center, at Edwards Air Force Base, California. As well as more thrust, the new engine has software modifications to ensure optimal engine performance and an auto-throttle capability. Changes within the engine itself include monolithic bladed disks (blisks) in the modular three-stage fan section, plus a new and more durable radial afterburner nozzle.

Phased Introduction

The first Block 60 F-16 took to the air at Fort Worth on 6 December 2003, with a phased development program that ensured the first aircraft could be handed over to the UAE even before the completion of system integration and flight testing. The UAE ordered 80 Block 60 aircraft, comprising 55

F-16E Block 60

Weight (maximum take-off): 20,865kg (46,000lbs)
Dimensions: Length 15.04m (49ft 4in); Wingspan 9.4488m (31ft); Height 5.09m (16ft 8.5in)
Powerplant: One General Electric F110-GE-132 turbofan
Maximum speed: Mach 2.02 at 40,000ft
Range: Maximum ferry range with external fuel: 3700km (2300 miles)
Ceiling: 18,000m (60,000ft)
Crew: 1
Armament: One M61A1 20mm (0.787in) cannon; six under-wing hardpoints, three fuselage hardpoints, two wingtip pylons: AIM-9 Sidewinder, AIM-7 Sparrow, AIM-120 AMRAAM, IRIS-T, Python 4 air-to-air missiles; ground attack: 70mm unguided rocket pods, AGM-65 Maverick missile, Mk82, Mk83, Mk84 bombs, BGU-39

F-16E BLOCK 60
A Lockheed Martin F-16E Block 60, 3056, serial number 00-6031, from the 1st Squadron, UAEAF.

F-16F Block 60

Weight (maximum take-off): 20,865kg (46,000lbs)

Dimensions: Length 15.04m (49ft 4in); Wingspan 9.4488m (31ft); Height 5.09m (16ft 8.5in)

Powerplant: One General Electric F110-GE-132 turbofan

Maximum speed: Mach 2.02 at 40,000ft

Range: Maximum ferry range with external fuel: 3700km (2300 miles)

Ceiling: 18,000m (60,000ft)

Crew: 2

Armament: One M61A1 20mm (0.787in) cannon; six under-wing hardpoints, three fuselage hardpoints, two wingtip pylons: AIM-9 Sidewinder, AIM-7 Sparrow, AIM-120 AMRAAM, IRIS-T, Python 4 air-to-air missiles; ground attack: 70mm unguided rocket pods, AGM-65 Maverick missile, Mk82, Mk83, Mk84 guided or unguided bombs, BGU-39 Small Diameter Bomb

single-seat F-16Es and 25 two-seat F-16Fs.

In this way, the initial Standard 0 aircraft began to be handed over in September 2004 to begin training of UAE aircrews in the United States. In May 2005, the first Standard 1 aircraft with basic operational capabilities was delivered. Standard 2 introduced terrain-following radar, additional electronic warfare modes and more weapons options. Finally, Standard 3, delivered from 2007, added a BAE Systems TERPROM digital terrain avoidance and navigation system.

The UAE's F-16E/F fleet is also notably well provided with air-to-air and air-to-ground weapons options, with the country acquiring 491 AIM-120B AMRAAMs, 267 AIM-9M Sidewinders, 163 AGM-88 HARMs, 52 AGM-84 Harpoons and 1163 AGM-65D/G Maverick air-to-ground missiles.

F-16F BLOCK 60

A Lockheed Martin F-16F Block 60, 3023 (serial number 00-6078), from the 2nd Squadron UAEAF.

Block 70/72

The latest F-16 production standard offered by Lockheed Martin is the Block 70/72. Among the features included in this configuration is the Northrop Grumman AN/APG-83 Scalable Agile Beam Radar (SABR), an AESA radar that is also being retrofitted on a number of older US Air Force F-16s.

The Block 70/72 also features an enhanced glass cockpit, including a large pedestal multifunction display, updated mission computers and an advanced electronic warfare suite. There is also provision for the Joint Helmet Mounted Cueing System (JHMCS). While the Block 70 configuration is powered by a General Electric F110 turbofan, Block 72s are powered by the Pratt & Whitney F100.

As well as the engine options – a carryover from the Block 30/32, Block 40/42 and Block 50/52 series

F-16V VIPER

Also known as Block 70 or 72, the F-16V represents an upgrade intended to enable the F-16 to operate in an environment where fifth-generation fighters are active. This includes a single all-functions computer to replace the previous three dedicated systems and an electronically scanned array radar. A 'glass cockpit', with all instrumentation displayed on multifunction LCD screens rather than physical readouts and gauges, allows the crew to reconfigure the information they receive whenever necessary. Advanced electronic systems enhance the situational awareness of the crew and provide capabilities unavailable to earlier generations of fighter aircraft. The latest air-to-air missiles can be launched 'over the shoulder' at targets behind the launching aircraft.

POLISH VIPER
A Polish Air Force F-16V Viper approaches a US Air Force KC-135 Stratotanker from the 100th Air Refueling Wing during Exercise Baltic Operations over Poland, June 2020.

Whilst dedicated aircraft may be more efficient in any given role, diversity comes at a price that goes beyond the initial purchase. For operators of small fleets of combat aircraft, it may simply be too expensive to maintain stocks of spares for each handful of different aircraft. The F-16V provides ground attack, maritime strike and air superiority capability in a single package, reducing purchase costs and maintenance overheads. An additional benefit is commonality and interoperability with the air forces of allied states.

– customers of the Block 70/72 can choose whether or not to have the 'big spine' modifications that are also found on other, earlier F-16s. The enlarged dorsal spine can accommodate additional avionics, communications systems, countermeasures and more. The Block 70/72 is also compatible with the range-extending CFT fuel tanks. Another major development that comes with the Block 70/72 is the relocation of the F-16 production effort from Fort Worth (now tasked with F-35 Lightning II manufacture) to Greenville, South Carolina.

The first new-build Block 70/72 aircraft – a two-seat F-16 in Block 70 configuration for Bahrain – made its maiden flight on 24 January 2023 at Greenville. The test pilots for the flight were Dwayne Opella and Monessa Balzhiser.

While the move to Greenville reflected the F-16's diminishing priority compared with the F-35, demand for the older jet has certainly not gone away, with 128 jets on order at the time of the Block 70's maiden flight. At the same time, six customers had already signed up for the Block 70/72: Bahrain, Bulgaria, Jordan, Morocco, Slovakia and Taiwan.

The New Viper
As well as the new-build Block 70/72 aircraft, Lockheed Martin continues to market an upgrade package for older jets, which can be brought up to a similar standard, known as F-16V ('V' for Viper). These aircraft incorporate an

avionics package based on that found in the Block 70/72 including the AN/APG-83 SABR radar. Other changes include new mission computers, navigation equipment, large colour multifunction displays, Advanced Identification Friend or Foe (AIFF) transponders, an updated electronic warfare suite and the Link 16 tactical datalink.

Importantly, the F-16V upgrade can also be introduced on older F-16A/B models, as is the case with Taiwan, for example, which was the first country to purchase the modernization package.

There is a limit to how far a given airframe can be upgraded whilst remaining cost-effective and combat-effective. However, the

F-16V is not the same aircraft as the F-16A/B or even the F-16C/D. With vastly better electronics, additional internal space and greater fuel capacity, recent models are not the lightweight, cheap fighters conceived in the 1970s; they are the product of a new century and well suited to current needs. It is true that the F-16 is a fourth-generation fighter in a world where fifth-generation aircraft are becoming more common. Yet it is sufficiently advanced and capable to be competitive and much cheaper alternative to the top-end fighters. In that, it retains the spirit of the original design. Current operators include the United States and the

F-16D(V) BLOCK 70

A Royal Bahraini Air Force Lockheed F-16D(V) Block 70, 1611, serial number 18-0011, circa 2023.

four original European partners: Belgium, Denmark, Netherlands and Norway. These include Greece, Portugal and Turkey.

The popularity of the F-16 is undiminished, with orders for new aircraft continuing and older examples being refurbished and upgraded or passed down the chain to new operators as they are replaced. It has been estimated that the F-16V will be in service into the 2070s, and that further-developed variants may at some point be offered. It is also possible that more overseas variants may appear, with manufacturers choosing to base their designs on the proven airframe, tailored to local needs and markets.

F-16D(V) Block 70

Weight (maximum take-off): 20,865kg (46,000lbs)
Dimensions: Length 15.02m (49ft 3in); Wingspan 9.449m (31ft); Height 5.09m (16ft 8.5in)
Powerplant: One Pratt and Whitney F100-PW-200/220/229 or General Electric F110-GE-100/129
Maximum speed: Mach 2 at 1219m (40,000ft)
Range: Maximum ferry range with external fuel: 3218km (2000 miles)
Ceiling: 18,000m (60,000ft)

Crew: 2
Armament: One M61A1 20mm (0.787in) cannon; six under-wing hardpoints, three fuselage hardpoints, two wingtip pylons: AIM-9 Sidewinder, AIM-7 Sparrow, AIM-120 AMRAAM, IRIS-T, Python 4 air-to-air missiles; ground attack: 70mm unguided rocket pods, AGM-65 Maverick missile; anti-radiation: AGM-45 Shrike, AGM-88 HARM missiles; maritime strike: AGM-84 Harpoon, AGM-119 Penguin missiles

TAKE-OFF
An F-16E Desert Falcon of the United
Arab Emirates Air Force launches out
of Nellis Air Force Base, Nevada.

United States operators

The US Air Force (USAF) has always been the most important operator of the F-16, with 2,230 production airframes having been delivered in successive versions, from the very first Block 1 jets to the advanced Block 52s.

The first F-16 for the US Air Force, a YF-16 prototype, was delivered to Edwards Air Force Base, California, for testing in January 1974, almost exactly a year before the General Dynamics design was selected as the service's new Lightweight Fighter (LWF).

FLIGHT TEST SQUADRON
An F-16D Fighting Falcon assigned to the 40th Flight Test Squadron flies a training mission off the Emerald Coast of Florida, United States, 2019.

Air Combat Command

After the eight Full-Scale Development (FSD) aircraft, the USAF announced plans to buy 650 F-16A/Bs, and the first series-production aircraft for the service began to roll out of General Dynamics' Fort Worth factory in August 1975. In 1977, the USAF announced it would buy another 783 F-16A/Bs.

The first production USAF F-16, an F-16A Block 1 aircraft, was accepted by the service in August 1978. This kickstarted deliveries of an eventual 768 F-16A/Bs for the service, comprising 43 Block 1, 73 Block 5, 213 Block 10 and 457 Block 15 aircraft. The last of these aircraft were completed in early 1985, after which production switched over exclusively to the F-16C/D.

The first of the F-16C/Ds for the USAF were Block 25 aircraft, production of which was launched in 1984, with the first example delivered to the service in July of that year. After around 1,500 of the Block 25 aircraft, production moved to the Block 40/42 version in 1990. From 1992, the more advanced Block 50/52 became the standard production version for the US Air Force.

Total production of the F-16C/D for the USAF amounted to 1,444 aircraft, comprising 244 Block 25, 407 Block 30, 62 Block 32, 266 Block 40, 196 Block 42, 216 Block 50 and 53 Block 52 aircraft. The last example to be delivered to the USAF was an F-16C Block 50, handed over in 2004.

The primary USAF operator is Air Combat Command (ACC), the successor to Tactical Air Command (TAC), which received its first F-16A at Hill Air Force Base, Utah, in January 1979, the recipient being the 388th Tactical Fighter Wing (TFW). It was a unit within this wing, the 4th Tactical Fighter Squadron (TFS), that became the first within the USAF to achieve initial operational capability (IOC) with the F-16, in November 1980.

As the ACC received more capable Block 40/42, and subsequently Block 50/52 aircraft, the command was able to cascade older Block 25 and 30/32 aircraft to Air Force Reserve Command (AFRC) and Air National Guard (ANG) units.

WEAPONS LOAD

A view of the weapons load on an F-16 from the 148th Fighter Wing, Minnesota Air National Guard, as it flies over the East Coast of the US.

Traditionally, the Block 25 and 30/32 aircraft were air defence specialists, with the LANTIRN-equipped Block 40/42 jets focusing on the ground-attack role and the specially equipped Block 50/52s flying defence-suppression missions with the AN/ASQ-213 HARM Targeting System (HTS). In practice, however, and especially since the uptick in operational deployments to Afghanistan and the Middle East, all versions and the different units operating them have increasingly undertaken the full spectrum of operations as required.

Common Configuration Implementation Program (CCIP)
A significant upgrade for the USAF's F-16 was the Common Configuration Implementation Program (CCIP), which was applied to some 650 Block 40/42/50/52 aircraft. CCIP brought these aircraft to a broadly similar standard and was undertaken in four phases, at the Ogden

Air Logistics Center at Hill Air Force Base. Phase 1 provided a new modular mission computer and colour multifunction cockpit displays. Phase 1A then added the AN/APX-113 interrogator/transponder (with the characteristic 'bird slicer' antenna in front of the cockpit), as well as the Lockheed Martin Sniper ATP imaging/targeting pod.

Under CCIP Phase 2, the upgraded F-16s received the Link 16 Multifunction Information Distribution System (MIDS) datalink, the Joint Helmet Mounted Cueing System (JHMCS) and an Electronic Horizontal Situation Indicator (EHSI).

Finally, Phase 3, which began at Ogden Air Logistics Center in 2005, saw the incorporation of Falcon STAR structural modifications. After upgrade, CCIP-modified aircraft are semi-officially designated as the F-16CM and F-16DM.

Aside from ACC, other major commands operate the F-16, namely the Pacific Air Forces

GROUND ATTACK
An F-16C assigned to the 522nd Fighter Squadron fires an AGM-65H Maverick air-to-ground missile at a target located over the Utah Test and Training Range.

(PACAF) and the United States Air Forces in Europe (USAFE).

Pacific Air Forces
After Tactical Air Command, PACAF was the next command to receive F-16s, with its initial unit being the 8th TFW at Kunsan Air Base in South Korea. The 8th TFW re-equipped with F-16s from May 1981, with the 35th and 80th TFS receiving the new jets to replace the F-4D Phantom II. The new PACAF unit was the 51st TFW at Osan Air Base, also in South Korea. Today, the 35th TFW at Misawa Air Base in Japan also flies F-16s, while an Alaska-based aggressor unit also falls within the PACAF area of responsibility. The latter is the 18th Aggressor Squadron (AGRS), which operates out of Elmendorf Air Force Base.

United States Air Forces in Europe

Significant numbers of F-16s were stationed in Europe during the final years of the Cold War to defend against possible Warsaw Pact aggression.

The first USAFE F-16 unit was the 50th TFW at Hahn Air Base in Germany, which, from July 1982, received F-16A/B Block 15 aircraft to replace its F-4Es. The 50th TFW's 313th TFS declared initial operational capability in December 1982. Before the fall of the Berlin Wall, other USAFE F-16 units had been established at Ramstein Air Base, Hahn Air Base and Spangdahlem Air Base, all in Germany, and at Torrejón Air Base in Spain. Today, however, only two USAFE bases continue to fly F-16: Spangdahlem Air Base in Germany and Aviano Air Base in Italy.

Air Force Reserve Command

In the mid-1980s, units of the Air Force Reserve Command (AFRC) began to receive F-16A/Bs, marking a break from previous policy that had seen older types cascaded down to reservist units from operational ones. The first AFRC F-16 unit was the 419th TFW at Hill Air Force Base, which began to receive Vipers in January 1984.

With the end of the Cold War, AFRC units saw extensive force reductions, but it remains as a backup force for the regular USAF, and its F-16s have been regularly deployed operationally, including to combat zones.

Air Force Materiel Command

Responsible for testing new weapon systems on USAF aircraft, including the F-16, the Air Force Materiel Command (AFMC) has long played a vital role in the Air Force's Viper community.

Through the years, different F-16s have regularly been used as test platforms for trials related to both the USAF Viper fleet, but also for other F-16 customers. The main hubs for this test are Edwards Air Force Base in California, Eglin Air Force Base in Florida and Hill Air Force Base in Utah.

AFMC units were the last to operate the older F-16A/B versions, including for photo-chase missions at Edwards Air Force Base. At the same time, the more capable F-16C/D versions were used for weapons integration and verification trials, including with the 46th Test Wing (TW) at Eglin Air Force Base.

Operational service

From the start, USAF F-16s were deployed overseas, putting them within closer reach of potential trouble spots in Europe and the Pacific. However, the combat debut of the F-16 in USAF hands came in the Middle East, with Operation Desert Storm in 1991, and the type

AIR-STRIKE MISSION
The pilot of a USAF F-16 looks over his right wing as he prepares to take off from Aviano Air Base, Italy, on an air-strike mission against targets in Yugoslavia in March 1999, during NATO Operation Allied Force.

AIR EDUCATION AND TRAINING COMMAND

Although the USAF's introduction of the F-35A has seen the demand for new F-16 pilots reduced, Air Education and Training Command (AETC) continues to provide F-16 training facilities for the service. Originally, Hill Air Force Base was the centre of USAF F-16 training, before responsibility switched to Luke Air Force Base, Arizona, and the resident 56th Fighter Wing (FW). As of mid-2023, only the 309th Fighter Squadron (FS) remains at Luke Air Force Base. It became the very last F-16 operator within the 56th FW once the joint US-Singapore F-16C/D unit – the 425th FS – relocated away from Luke.

With the 56th FW rationalized on a single F-16 squadron, much of the Viper training effort has moved to Holloman Air Force Base in New Mexico, along with training squadrons in Tucson and in San Antonio, Texas.

has been committed to operations in the same region with regularity ever since.

Desert Storm was launched with the aim of removing Saddam Hussein's Iraqi invasion force from Kuwait, and the F-16 was deployed in the operation in larger numbers than any other USAF fighter jet. In all, 249 F-16As and F-16Cs were committed to the campaign. With only a limited number of LANTIRN pods available, most USAF F-16s flew missions in daylight hours and delivered unguided munitions.

Despite the end of Desert Storm, USAF F-16s remained committed in the Middle East. Under Operations Northern Watch and Southern Watch, the aircraft were used to police no-fly zones established over Iraq. It was during a Southern Watch sortie on 27 December 1992 that an F-16D flown by Lt. Col. Gary North made history as the first USAF F-16 to score an air-to-air victory. This was also the first kill for the AIM-120 AMRAAM, which was used to

down an Iraqi MiG-25 Foxbat. In the 1990s, USAF F-16s were also involved in combat missions over the former Yugoslavia during Operation Allied Force. This campaign involved F-16s from both the USAF and from European air forces. Between them, these aircraft flew close air support, strike, reconnaissance, defence suppression and other missions.

After the 9/11 terror attacks on the United States, F-16s began to fly defensive missions over North America under Operation Enduring Freedom and later Operation Noble Eagle. In particular, defensive alerts were stepped up around New York City and Washington DC, although other bases around North America also increased their alert levels.

The events of 11 September 2001 also led to the next major combat engagement for the USAF F-16: Operation Enduring Freedom over Afghanistan. As a coalition of forces took on Taliban insurgents, F-16s were at the forefront of close air support missions.

USAF F-16s also returned to combat over Iraq in 2003 during Operation Iraqi Freedom. Subsequently, they participated in the enforcement of a no-fly zone over Libya as part of Operation Odyssey Dawn, alongside other NATO Viper operators.

Air National Guard
Today, the Air National Guard (ANG) is the largest operator of the F-16. While its primary responsibility is the defence of the continental United States, it also regularly deploys its F-16s on operations and exercises around the world.

The decision to field F-16s with the ANG, announced in March 1982, was a significant one, marking the expansion of the Guard as a credible fighting force operating the same equipment as its frontline counterparts.

From July 1983, the 169th Tactical Fighter Group (TFG) of the South Carolina ANG was the first Guard unit to receive F-16s, replacing its A-7D Corsair IIs.

Beginning in 1986, F-16s were assigned to ANG air defence units, starting with the 158th TFG of the Vermont ANG, which replaced its F-4Ds with the new fighter. With the assumption of air defence duties with the Viper, the ANG also began to receive the ADF version of the F-16, capable of launching the AIM-7 Sparrow air-to-air missile, which was coupled with an improved AN/APG-66 radar. The first modified F-16 Block 15 ADF variant was delivered to the Oregon ANG's 114th Tactical Fighter Training Squadron in early 1989.

US Navy service

With a requirement for an advanced aggressor aircraft to conduct dissimilar air combat training (DACT), the US Navy selected a special version of the F-16, the F-16N (for Navy). The aircraft was something of a hybrid, with a strengthened and lightened airframe based on the F-16C/D Block 30 but with the older AN/APG-66 radar from the F-16A/B. The M61A1 cannon was also removed to save weight. These aircraft were powered by F110-GE-100 engines.

The US Navy announced its selection of the F-16 for adversary work in January 1985 and placed orders for 22 single-seat F-16Ns and four two-seat TF-16N trainers. Deliveries took place between 1987 and 1988, and these aircraft served with squadrons at Naval Air

F-16C FIGHTING FALCON
Weight (maximum take-off): 19,187kg (42,300lb)
Dimensions: Length 15.04m (49ft 4in); Wingspan 9.4488m (31ft 3in); Height 5.09m (16ft 8.5in)
Powerplant: One General Electric F110-GE-100 turbofan
Maximum Speed: Mach 2.02 at 40,000ft
Range: Maximum ferry range with external fuel: 3862km (2400 miles)
Ceiling: 16,764m (55,000ft)
Crew: 1
Armament: One 20mm (0.787in) M61A1 six-barrel rotary cannon, plus up to 7700kg (17,000lb) of disposable stores carried on six hardpoints

F-16C BLOCK 25E
This F-16C, 84-0301, dating from 2014, was assigned to 64th Aggressor Squadron, 57th Adversary Tactics Group, Nellis AFB, wearing Blizzard camouflage marked for Colonel Dean Cadwell.

F-16C BLOCK 25A
Dating from 1988, this F-16C, 83-1128, served with the 422nd Test and Evaluation Squadron, 57th Fighter Weapons Wing. The aircraft is painted in a Europe 1 scheme.

F-16C BLOCK 30
This F-16C, 86-0295, was assigned to 18th Agressor Squadron,
354th Fighter Wing, Eielson Air Force Base, Alaska, in 2018.

F-16CM BLOCK 42G
This F-16CM, 89-2112, was assigned to the 112th Fighter
Squadron, 180th Fighter Wing, Ohio Air National Guard,
Toledo, in 2017. It is finished in a grey "Have Glass" camouflage.

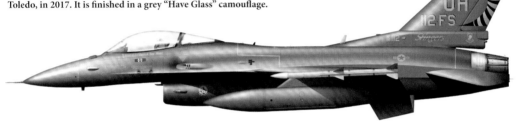

F-16C BLOCK 40
Dating from 2021, this F-16C, 89-2060, was assigned to 8th Fighter
Wing "Wolf Pack", Kunsan Air Force Base, South Korea. It is wearing
the "three greys" camouflage, marked for Colonel John Gallemore.

F-16C BLOCK 32D
This F-16C, 86-0272, served with the 64th Aggressor Squadron,
57th Adversary Tactics Group, Nellis AFB in 2017, wearing
"Shark" camouflage scheme marked for Captain Justin Bellamy.

REFUELLING
A 401st Tactical Fighter Wing F-16C refuels from a KC-135 Stratotanker aircraft as another F-16 stands by during Operation Desert Storm, 1991.

Station Miramar, California, Naval Air Station Key West, Florida, and Naval Air Station Oceana, Virginia.

Even though the F-16Ns received structural modifications to cope with the rigours of air combat manoeuvring, they began to show signs of metal fatigue relatively soon, forcing them to be withdrawn from service prematurely. The aircraft were finally retired in 1994.

With the withdrawal of the F-16Ns, the US Navy was left without a high-performance aggressor aircraft, but a windfall was provided in the shape of a batch of F-16s that had been manufactured for Pakistan but were subsequently embargoed.

A total of 14 F-16 Block 15 OCU aircraft were taken from the Aircraft Maintenance And Regeneration Center (AMARC) at Davis–Monthan Air Force Base, Arizona, and then delivered to the US Navy for adversary work.

Since then, the US Navy has moved to further increase its fleet of F-16 aggressor jets. In 2021, the service announced that it would be receiving 20 single-seat F-16C Block 32 aircraft and six two-seat F-16D Block 25 aircraft. These were transferred to the Navy as the USAF retired them under a scheme to divest 124 F-16s by 2026, with the Air Force now consolidating on Block 40 and above.

European Operators

In what became known as the 'Sale of the Century', considerable numbers of F-16A/B aircraft were sold to European NATO countries in a process kickstarted by Belgium, Denmark, the Netherlands and Norway – collectively, the European Participating Air Forces (EPAF). All four of these nations had previously operated the F-104 Starfighter, and the F-16 provided a tremendous advance in capability, with the agility to take on the latest generation of Soviet-made fighters that, as of the early 1980s, were the primary adversary for NATO in Europe. Subsequently, the European F-16 community became larger still, although many of the continent's operators are in the process of retiring their now-aging Vipers, to be replaced by the fifth-generation F-35.

INTERNATIONAL SECURITY ASSISTANCE
FORCE (ISAF) MISSON
A Royal Netherlands Air Force F-16 flies a
combat mission over Afghanistan, June 2009.

Belgium

As one of the first four export customers for the F-16, Belgium ordered a total of 160 F-16A/Bs in two batches; of the surviving aircraft, 86 were eventually put through the Mid-Life Update (MLU) programme, emerging with the semi-official designation F-16AM/BM. These are now coming to the end of their career, however, with a much-reduced fleet (accelerated by the transfer of aircraft to Jordan) continuing in service pending the introduction of the F-35A.

Under the terms of the EPAF arrangement, F-16s for the first four European NATO operators were built locally in Belgium and the Netherlands. In Belgium's case, manufacture was handled by SABCA, which also produced aircraft for Denmark. Meanwhile, F100 engines for the EPAF F-16s were produced by Fabrique Nationale (also in Belgium). Ultimately, EPAF produced 524 F-16s.

The first Belgian order was for 116 aircraft – 96 single-seat F-16As and 20 two-seat F-16Bs. The first Belgian-built F-16 made its maiden flight on 11 December 1978 and was accepted in January 1979,

becoming the first locally built F-16 to be delivered to a European operator. SABCA-built aircraft, initially Block 1 and Block 5 aircraft, eventually reached a Block 10 standard following a process of modifications. Production then switched to Block 15, and the last of the initial batch of 116 aircraft was delivered in May 1985.

Meanwhile, Belgium had ordered another 44 aircraft (40 F-16As and four F-16Bs) that were completed to Block 15OCU standard.

Belgian F-16s feature some specific local modifications and stores. Instead of an external electronic countermeasures pod, some of the Belgian jets were fitted with an internal system, known as Carapace, which adds a distinctive fairing under the intake as well as radar warning receivers (RWRs) in the drag chute compartment. For the reconnaissance role, Belgian F-16s were made compatible with the Per Udsen (now Terma)

BELGIAN F-16A BLOCK 20 MLU
A SABCA (Sociétés Anonyme Belge de Constructions Aéronautiques)-built F-16A Block 20 MLU, FA-101, serial number 86-0077, Belgian Air Force, 1st Squadron, circa 2007.

F-16A Block 20 MLU
Weight (maximum take-off): 17,009.71kg (37,500lbs) maximum takeoff
Dimensions: Length 15.14m (49ft 8in); Wingspan 9,97m (32ft 8in); Height 4.9m (16ft 1in)
Powerplant: One Pratt & Whitney F100-PW-220 turbofan
Maximum speed: 1472.55km/h (915mph) at sea level
Range: 1166.77km (725 miles)
Ceiling: 6598.92m (21,650ft)
Crew: 1
Armament: One M61A1 20mm (0.787in) cannon (500 rd); six hardpoints: AIM-9 Sidewinder, AIM-7 Sparrow, AIM-120 AMRAAM air-to-air missiles; AGM-65 Maverick missile, GBU-31 (JDAM) 2000lb guided bomb, GBU-38 (JDAM) 500lb guided bomb

DANISH F-16B

A SABCA (Sociétés Anonyme Belge de Constructions Aéronautiques)-built
Danish Air Force F-16B, serial number ET-206.

Modular Reconnaissance Pod (MRP), which replaced the previous Orpheus pod. Another product from Terma, the Pylon Integrated Dispenser Stations (PIDS), is also used by Belgian F-16s.

The end of the Cold War saw Belgium greatly reduce its frontline combat fleet, with many F-16s put into storage, resulting in an operational force of 72 aircraft plus 18 operational reserves.

With the selection of the F-35A as the F-16's successor, the drawdown has continued. As of 2023, the Belgian Air Force flies around 50 F-16s. With the first F-35s due to arrive in Belgium in 2025 and initial operating capability not expected until mid-2027, F-16s will remain the primary Belgian combat jets for some time to come.

As well as the Baltic Air Policing mission to protect the airspace of Estonia, Latvia and Lithuania, Belgian F-16s have taken part in successive combat operations since Operation Allied Force over Yugoslavia in 1999. These have included operations in Afghanistan, the Middle East and over Libya as part of the coalition against the so-called Islamic State.

Denmark

As one of the EPAF nations, Denmark acquired a total of 77 F-16A/B aircraft in two main batches, plus additional attrition replacement orders. Like the other EPAF operators, Denmark will replace its F-16s with F-35As.

The first order for the Royal Danish Air Force comprised 46 single-seat F-16As and 12 two-seat F-16B, which came from the SABCA production line in Belgium, completed to Block 1 standards. The first of these to be delivered, an F-16B, was handed over in January 1980. All 56 of these Block 1 aircraft were later upgraded to Block 10 standards under the Pacer Loft programme carried out in Denmark.

Denmark then placed a follow-on order for 12 Block 15 aircraft (eight F-16As and four F-16Bs) in August 1984. Unlike the first batch of Danish deliveries, these aircraft were built by Fokker in the Netherlands. Two batches of attrition replacements then followed: three former US Air Force Block 15 aircraft, delivered to Denmark in 1994, and a batch of four more Block 10/15s, received in 1997.

Specific features of the Danish F-16 include a searchlight for night interceptions. Fitted in the port forward fuselage side in front of the canopy, it was also found on the Norwegian jets. The no. 3 and no. 7 wing stations are adapted to accommodate the Terma Pylon Integrated Dispenser Stations (PIDS), which carry chaff cartridges and are also used by Belgium. These are operated as part of an integrated countermeasures suite, controlled by Terma's Electronic Warfare Management System (EWMS). Reconnaissance pods used by Danish F-16s include the Per Udsen (now Terma)

FOKKER F-16B Block 20

Weight (maximum take-off): 17,009.71kg (37,500lbs) maximum takeoff

Dimensions: Length 14.6m (47ft 11in); Wingspan 9.5m (31ft 2in); Height 5m (16ft 5in)

Powerplant: One Pratt & Whitney F100-PW-220 turbofan

Maximum speed: 1472.55km/h (915mph) at sea level

Range: 3218km (2000 miles)

Ceiling: 6598.92m (21,650ft)

Crew: 2

Armament: One M61A1 20mm (0.787in) cannon (500 rd); six hardpoints: AIM-9 Sidewinder, AIM-7 Sparrow, AIM-120 AMRAAM air-to-air missiles; AGM-65 Maverick missile, GBU-31 (JDAM) 2000lb guided bomb

NORWEGIAN FOKKER F-16B
A Fokker F-16B Block 20 MLU, 304 (serial number 78-0304), Royal Norwegian Air Force, circa 2006.

Modular Reconnaissance Pod (MRP), which replaced the earlier Red Baron pod. As an EPAF member, Denmark took part in the MLU programme and provided these modifications to 61 F-16s, with work completed locally in Aalborg. International operations in which Danish F-16s have been involved include 'Allied Force' in 1999, 'Enduring Freedom' over Afghanistan in 2002–03, 'Baltic Air Policing', and 'Iceland Air Policing and Surveillance', with a first deployment to Iceland in 2009.

As of 2023, the Royal Danish Air Force operates around 43 F-16AM/BMs but received its first F-35A in April of that year. While this aircraft was delivered to Luke Air Force Base, Arizona, for training, the first F-35 operations in Denmark are also slated for 2023, kickstarting the replacement of the F-16.

Norway
Another of the European Participating Air Forces (EPAF)

F-16 customers, the Royal Norwegian Air Force (RNoAF), placed orders for 74 F-16A/B aircraft (60 F-16As and 12 F-16Bs), of which 56 were eventually updated under the MLU programme. With relatively rapid deliveries of F-35As, the RNoAF was able to withdraw its F-16 fleet entirely in early 2022. Of the retired aircraft, 32 are being transferred to Romania, where they will replace that country's MiG-21 Lancers. Up to 12 Norwegian F-16s were also acquired by Draken International, the US-based adversary air provider.

Together with Belgium, Denmark and the Netherlands, Norway ordered the F-16 in July 1975, establishing in the process a European consortium to assemble the aircraft under licence. F-16s for Norway were delivered from the Fokker production line in the Netherlands between 1980 and 1984.

The first RNoAF F-16 made its maiden flight in December 1979, and the early aircraft were completed to Block 1 and Block 5 standard (later upgraded to Block 10). In addition, two more F-16B Block 15s were ordered as attrition replacements, these being produced by General Dynamics in the United States.

FOKKER F-16A Block 20

Weight (maximum take-off): 17,009.71kg (37,500lbs) maximum takeoff

Dimensions: Length 15.14m (49ft 8in); Wingspan 9.97m (32ft 8in); Height 4.9m (16ft 1in)

Powerplant: One Pratt & Whitney F100-PW-220 turbofan

Maximum speed: 1472.55km/h (915mph) at sea level

Range: 1166km (725 miles)

Ceiling: 6598.92m (21,650ft)

Crew: 1

Armament: One M61A1 20mm (0.787in) cannon (500 rd); six hardpoints: AIM-9 Sidewinder, AIM-7 Sparrow, AIM-120 AMRAAM air-to-air missiles; AGM-65 Maverick missile, GBU-31 (JDAM) 2000lb guided bomb

With very specific operational requirements in Norway, the RNoAF jets featured certain modifications, including being the first F-16s to be fitted with braking parachutes. Located inside a large rectangular extension at the base of the tail fin, these proved necessary for operations on short and snow-covered runways, as often found at dispersed sites. Norwegian F-16s were also fitted with Danish F-16s, used for night-time interceptions.

Other specific features of the Norwegian F-16s included the ability to launch the locally developed Kongsberg Penguin anti-ship missile. This was delivered from 1987 and features combined inertial and infrared guidance. The 56 aircraft that passed through the MLU programme comprised 45 F-16As and 11 F-16Bs, and work was completed in December 2001.

Norway took its F-16s to war

NETHERLANDS F-16A
A Fokker F-16A Block 20 MLU, J-016 (serial number 89-0016), Royal Netherlands Air Force, 312 Squadron, circa 2012.

for the first time over the former Yugoslavia during Operation Allied Force in 1999, with the jets being deployed to Grazzanise in Italy. The RNoAF later took part in Operation Enduring Freedom over Afghanistan, flying from Kyrgyzstan alongside aircraft from the Netherlands and Denmark. Norway also took part in the Baltic Air Policing mission with its F-16s. The aircraft went to war again in 2011, over Libya, during the NATO-led Unified Protector operation.

Netherlands

The Netherlands was one of the first four European Participating Air Forces (EPAF) to sign up for the F-16 as part of the so-called 'Sale of the Century', primarily to replace its ageing F-104 fleet – including in the tactical nuclear strike role. The Dutch became one of the most enthusiastic operators of the F-16, eventually purchasing 213 F-16A/B versions, some of which were built locally by Fokker. While surviving jets were upgraded to MLU standard, fleet numbers began to be reduced with the end of the Cold War, and this process

NATO PATROL

A Royal Netherlands Air Force F-16 Fighting Falcon aircraft conducts a mission over Afghanistan, May 2008, after receiving fuel from a USAF KC-135R Stratotanker aircraft.

continued steadily in the years that followed.

As of early 2023, all remaining active Royal Netherlands Air Force (RNLAF) F-16s were located at a single base, Volkel, where the local frontline fleet was down to around 24 aircraft, with another 18 examples held in reserve, pending full replacement by the F-35A. In the meantime, surplus Dutch F-16s have been sold to Chile and Jordan and to the contractor adversary company Draken International.

The Netherlands' first order was for 102 F-16s, comprising 80 single-seat F-16As and 22 two-seat

F-16Bs, to be assembled by Fokker. The first Dutch-built F-16 took to the air on 3 May 1979, and an initial delivery to the RNLAF followed in June of the same year.

In December 1983, the Dutch government approved plans to buy another 111 F-16s (97 F-16As and 14 F-16Bs), making up a total fleet of 213 aircraft (minus attrition in the interim). The last of these 213 aircraft rolled out of the Fokker production facility in February 1992.

Some of the Dutch F-16s were equipped for reconnaissance duties, carrying the Orpheus pod that had been used by the RF-104G. Modified aircraft received the semi-official F-16A(R) designation. The older Orpheus pod, with optical cameras and an infrared line scanner, was later replaced by the Medium Altitude Reconnaissance System (MARS). This can be

integrated on any RNLAF F-16 via the Per Udsen Modular Reconnaissance Pod (MRP).

In 1993, as part of the post-Cold War defence drawdown, it was decided that only 138 of the jets would pass through the MLU programme rather than the 170 originally planned. By 2003, all remaining operational Dutch F-16s had undergone the MLU. The same year, however, saw another major reduction in the fleet, with the decision to reduce numbers by 25 per cent. This move also freed up F-16s to be sold to other operators. Beginning in 2005, Jordan acquired six F-16BMs, while Chile acquired their first batch of 18 jets (11 F-16AMs and seven F-16BMs) in the same year. This was followed by another batch of 18 single-seaters in 2008. Dutch F-16s have been widely deployed on operations, beginning with missions over the former Yugoslavia in the 1990s under Operation Joint Falcon and Operation Allied Force. During the latter campaign, on 4 April 1999, a Dutch F-16 shot down a Serbian MiG-29 fighter with an AIM-120 AMRAAM missile, in the first RNLAF aerial kill since World War II. Dutch F-16s also struck Serbian ground targets in the same operation, including using AGM-65G Maverick air-to-ground missiles.

The RNLAF flew missions over Afghanistan under Operation Enduring Freedom, with F-16s initially based in Kyrgyzstan. Subsequently, the jest also took part in counter-Daesh missions in the Middle East. Regular deployments have also been made to the Baltics as part of NATO's Baltic Air Policing rotational mission to defend the airspace of Estonia, Latvia and Lithuania.

Greece

Greece received 170 F-16s of various types between 1989 and 2010. With a large-scale modernization programme underway, these aircraft will remain the backbone of the Hellenic Air Force's combat fleet for many years to come. Roughly 150 Greek Vipers were still operational as of 2023, of which 84 aircraft – all of them the more capable Block 52+ and Block 52+ Advanced jets – are being brought up to F-16V standard.

Greece announced plans to buy the F-16 in November 1984, shortly after regional rival Turkey had done the same. At first, Greece acquired 34 F-16Cs and six F-16Ds to replace its ageing Northrop F-5A Freedom Fighters. However, it was not until January 1987 that a formal contract was agreed. This was for Peace Xenia I, a Foreign Military Sales deal involving F110-powered Block 30 aircraft. The first

of these, an F-16D, was handed over to Athens at Fort Worth in November 1988. Deliveries were completed in October 1989.

In April 1993, another Greek F-16 order was placed under the Peace Xenia II programme. This involved another 40 F-16C/D aircraft completed to the more capable Block 50 standard. The breakdown was made up of 32 F-16Cs and eight F-16Ds, again with the F110 engine. The first two aircraft from this deal – a single-seater and a two-seater – were rolled out at Fort Worth in January 1997, with formal handover of the first aircraft following in May of the same year and a ferry flight to Greece involving the first four aircraft in July. A planned order for 20 more Block

GREEK F-16D
A Hellenic Air Force F-16D stands on the runway. Deliveries of the F-16D to Greece began in 1989.

30 aircraft, to be sourced second-hand and to replace the Hellenic Air Force's Vought A-7 Corsair IIs, was abandoned. Instead, the next Greek order, under Peace Xenia III, was a more ambitious acquisition, intended to strengthen the air arm in the face of continued Turkish Air Force expansion.

In 2000, after looking at several other advanced and costly fighter options, Athens ordered 50 F-16 Block 52+ aircraft, followed by 60 the year after. These were to be provided in the form of 40 single-seat F-16Cs and 20 two-seat F-16Ds. All were compatible with Conformal Fuel Tanks (CFTs). The last Peace Xenia III aircraft was delivered to Greece in June 2004.

After scrapping plans to purchase the Eurofighter Typhoon, the Greek government instead opted for another Viper order, under Peace Xenia IV, to finally replace the veteran fleet of A-7s. This deal covered 20 F-16C and 10 F-16D Block 52+ Advanced versions, also sometimes referred to as Block 52M aircraft, and was signed in December 2005, with a

total estimated cost of around $3.1 billion.

Greece's F-16s can carry the Collins Aerospace DB-110 reconnaissance pod and pack a powerful punch in terms of air-to-ground ordnance. Options include the AGM-154C Joint Stand-Off Weapon (JSOW), Joint Direct Attack Munition (JDAM) and – reportedly – the Wind Corrected Munitions Dispenser (WCMD).

The older F-16 Block 30s are now consolidated with a single squadron: 330 Mira. These aircraft have undergone the Falcon UP service-life extension, work being undertaken locally by Hellenic Aerospace Industry (HAI). This work has increased the lifetime of each aircraft from 4000 to 8000 hours.

In terms of operational activity, the Greek F-16 fleet has, over the years, been repeatedly engaged in encounters and even dogfights with the Turkish Air Force over the Aegean Sea. At times, these incidents have pitted Greek F-16s against Turkish ones, although most details remain highly disputed as well as classified.

Italy

The Italian Air Force only operated the F-16 relatively briefly and as an interim fighter. This was following the withdrawal of the F-104S Starfighter and prior to the service entry of the Typhoon (known as the F-2000 in Italian service).

F-16C BLOCK 50

Weight (maximum take-off): 19,187kg (42,300lb)
Dimensions: Length 15.06m (49ft 5in), Wingspan 9.448m (31ft), Height 5.09m (16ft 8in)
Powerplant: One General Electric F110-GE-100 turbofan
Maximum speed: Mach 2.05
Range: 579km (360 miles)
Ceiling: 16,764m (55,000ft)
Crew: 1
Armament: One 20mm (0.787in) M61A1 six-barrel rotary cannon, plus up to 7700kg (17,000lb) of disposable stores carried on six hardpoints

F-16C BLOCK 50
Greece was a major customer for the F-16C Block 50, illustrated here.

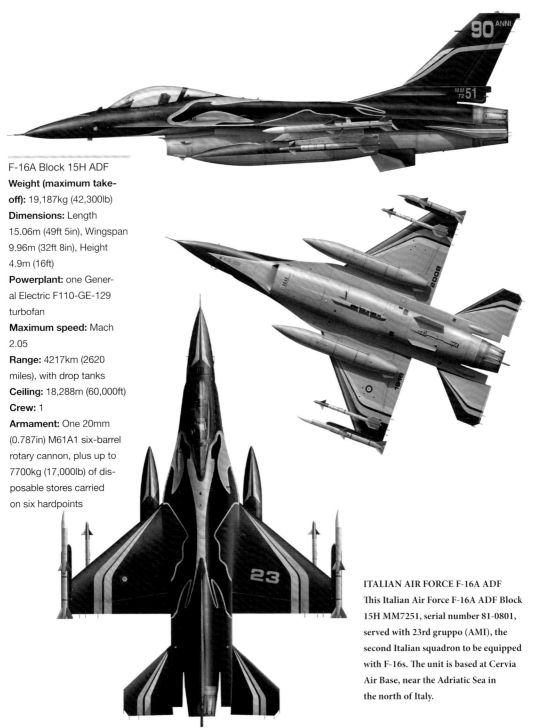

F-16A Block 15H ADF

Weight (maximum take-off): 19,187kg (42,300lb)

Dimensions: Length 15.06m (49ft 5in), Wingspan 9.96m (32ft 8in), Height 4.9m (16ft)

Powerplant: one General Electric F110-GE-129 turbofan

Maximum speed: Mach 2.05

Range: 4217km (2620 miles), with drop tanks

Ceiling: 18,288m (60,000ft)

Crew: 1

Armament: One 20mm (0.787in) M61A1 six-barrel rotary cannon, plus up to 7700kg (17,000lb) of disposable stores carried on six hardpoints

ITALIAN AIR FORCE F-16A ADF
This Italian Air Force F-16A ADF Block 15H MM7251, serial number 81-0801, served with 23rd gruppo (AMI), the second Italian squadron to be equipped with F-16s. The unit is based at Cervia Air Base, near the Adriatic Sea in the north of Italy.

Prior to operating the F-16 as a stopgap solution, Italy also leased 24 Tornado ADV interceptors from the United Kingdom.

In March 2001, under the Peace Caesar programme, Italy signed a lease on 34 F-16A/B aircraft from the United States. Thirty of these jets were Block 15 Air Defense Fighters (ADF), while the remainder comprised three F-16B Block 5/10 aircraft and a single F-16B ADF. Four other airframes were provided for use as spare parts.

The Peace Caesar lease ran for five years (with an option for another five), and the aircraft were delivered between July 2003 and November 2004. Each aircraft was taken out of storage in the United States and then fully refurbished before delivery, with modifications including the Falcon UP service-life extension. Once the F-2000 became available, Italy was able to withdraw its F-16s. The last operating unit, the 18° Gruppo at Trapani-Birgi in Sicily, was disbanded in May 2012.

Slovakia
In 2018, Slovakia ordered 14 new-build F-16 Block 70 fighters

TURKISH F-16C BLOCK 50
A Turkish Aerospace Industries-built F-16C Block 50, serial number 93-0671, Turkish Air Force, 152 Filo, circa 2006. 152 Filo converted to the F-16 in 1999. It was one of the last Turkish squadrons to convert to the Fighting Falcon.

from the United States to replace its MiG-29 fleet. The Vipers will incorporate advanced features including the AN/APG-83 active electronically scanned array (AESA) radar, a modernized cockpit and Conformal Fuel Tanks. The first aircraft are expected to be delivered in 2024. Ahead of this, Slovakia took the decision to transfer 13 of its MiG-29s to Ukraine for use in the war with Russia.

Turkey
Turkey operates the world's third largest F-16 fleet, with a total of 270 aircraft having been delivered in successively more capable Block 30, Block 50 and Block 50+ configurations. Most of these aircraft were assembled locally by Turkish Aerospace Industries (TAI). This company was also responsible for the production

F-16C BLOCK 50
Weight (maximum take-off): 19,187kg (42,300lb)
Dimensions: Length 15.06m (49ft 5in), Wingspan 9.448m (31ft), Height 5.09m (16ft 8in)
Powerplant: One General Electric F110-GE-100 turbofan
Maximum speed: Mach 2.05
Range: 579km (360 miles)
Ceiling: 16,764m (55,000ft)
Crew: 1
Armament: One 20mm (0.787in) M61A1 six-barrel rotary cannon, plus up to 7700kg (17,000lb) of disposable stores carried on six hardpoints

of centre/aft fuselage sections and wings.

As of 2023, approximately 245 of the jets remain in use, and Turkey has chosen to upgrade 35 of its oldest Block 30 jets, reflecting their continued importance.

The first phase of Turkish F-16 procurement was the Peace Onyx I programme launched in September

1983. This covered 136 F-16Cs and 24 F-16Ds, of which the first 44 were completed to Block 30 standard. The next 116 aircraft within Peace Onyx I were Block 40-standard jets that included the provision for LANTIRN pods. The Block 40 aircraft also feature APG-68(V) radar, GPS navigation, automatic terrain-following capability, digital flight controls, revised countermeasures dispensers and the ability to carry AIM-120 AMRAAM missiles.

The first eight aircraft from Peace Onyx I were built at Fort Worth, with assembly of the remainder handled by TAI in Turkey. Deliveries took place from 1987, and the first two F-16C assembly kits were handed over in March. An official handover ceremony followed in July of the same year. In 1994, TAI began the Falcon-Up structural modification programme on the Peace Onyx I

aircraft. Peace Onyx II, signed in March 1992, covered 60 F-16C and 20 F-16D Block 50 aircraft which were delivered between 1996 and 1999. The Turkish Block 50s were provided with the AGM-88 HARM anti-radiation missile for the role of defence suppression. Deliveries of these aircraft took place from 1996 to 1997.

The Peace Onyx III contract provided another batch of 40 F-16C/Ds. Intended as attrition replacements, these aircraft were delivered between 1998 and 1999.

As well as HARM capability, the Block 50 aircraft have APG-68(V5) radar, a secure-voice communication system and new radar warning receivers.

The most recent Peace Onyx IV deal, signed in May 2007, provided another 14 F-16C and 16 F-16D Block 50+ jets. These jets are compatible with the X (kg) (1,300lb) Roketsan Stand-

Off Missile (SOM) for standoff precision strike, as well as other indigenous weapons. These aircraft were delivered between June 2011 and December 2012.

Turkish F-16s have been subject to the Common Configuration Implementation Program (CCIP) upgrade, which added more sophisticated weapons and sensors, improved logistics support and reduced life cycle costs. Lockheed Martin provided a total of 163 CCIP kits for Turkey's surviving F-16C/D Block 40/50s. After modernization, the aircraft featured APG-68(V)9 multi-mode radar, colour cockpit displays and recorders, Joint Helmet Mounted Cueing System (JHMCS), Link 16

TURKISH F-16D

A Turkish Air Force General Dynamics F-16D Fighting Falcon CN HD-16 takes off from Konya Airport, Turkey, during Anatolian Eagle Air Force Exercise.

data link, Sniper targeting pods, and new weapons, including the AGM-84K Joint Standoff Land Attack Missile – Expanded Response (SLAM-ER), AGM-154A/C Joint Standoff Weapon (JSOW), AIM-9X Sidewinder and CBU-103/105 Wind Corrected Munitions Dispensers (WCMD). The DB-110 reconnaissance pod is also used.

More recently, TAI has set about upgrading 35 of its oldest Block 30 Vipers. This is based around a service life extension using kits supplied by Lockheed Martin.

As well as ongoing upgrades, there have been repeated reports that Ankara might also seek to buy another batch of new F-16s from the United States. With Turkey having been ejected from the F-35 program on account of its buying Russian S-400 air defence systems, the role of the F-16 to the Turkish Air Force is now even more important.

With tensions between Greece and Turkey an ever-present factor in the eastern Mediterranean, neither of these countries can be considered a likely candidate to provide F-16s to Ukraine despite their relatively large fleet sizes.

In 1999, the Turkish F-16 fleet saw operational service during Operation Allied Force over the former Yugoslavia. Missions were flown from home bases as well as Aviano in Italy. Both combat air patrol and precision attack sorties were flown. Turkish F-16s have also been involved in the long-running campaign against the Kurdistan Workers' Party (PKK), and the aircraft have also been involved in various encounters with the Hellenic Air Force over the Aegean Sea.

Romania

After Poland, Romania became the next F-16 operator in Eastern Europe. The NATO country has taken a unique approach to

building its F-16 fleet by gradually increasing its numbers, firstly with a batch of 12 second-hand jets from Portuguese stocks, followed by another five from the same source, and finally 32 more second-hand aircraft from Norway.

In mid-2023, the Romanian Air Force finally retired its MiG-21 LanceR fleet, leaving the F-16 as the sole combat jet operated by the country. Initially, there was speculation that Israel would provide Romania with second-hand F-16A/Bs. Belgium was viewed as another possibility. Meanwhile, in 2008, the US Congress also approved a potential sale of 48 F-16s – 24 new-build F-16C/D Block 50/52 aircraft along

ROMANIAN F-16AM
A Romanian Air Force F-16AM
Fighting Falcon from Escadrila 53
performs a demonstration flight
at Vadeni Fly-In air show, Brăila,
Romania, May 2018.

with 24 refurbished surplus US Air Force F-16C/D Block 25 jets.

In the event, Romania opted for second-hand jets from Portugal, and the Peace Carpathian I deal of 2016 covered the batch of F-16s: nine single-seat F-16As and three two-seat F-16Bs. All aircraft were MLU-upgraded. In this way, the transfer of F-16s was unique, with the aircraft that had previously served with the US Air Force before being sold to Portugal becoming Romania's third frontline operator. Deliveries rook place between 2016 and 2017.

In 2020, Peace Carpathian II added another five F-16As to the Romanian fleet, with Portugal again supplying them. Deliveries were completed between 2020 and 2021. With the MiG-21 LanceR headed for retirement, Romania had a requirement for more F-16s and, under Peace Carpathian III

in 2022, acquired 32 former Royal Norwegian Air Force (RNaF) aircraft. This deal was finally approved in 2023, although the exact breakdown of variants to be supplied is unclear.

Portugal

While Portugal is a member of the European Participating Air Forces (EPAF), it was a relatively late entrant – a Letter of Acceptance (LOA) for the F-16 was signed only in August 1990. This kicked off a procurement process that led to an eventual total of 45 F-16A/B Block 15OCU aircraft being delivered to the Portuguese Air Force. The fleet has subsequently been reduced, including through transfers of aircraft to Romania. However, all surviving Portuguese jets have been brought up to MLU standard.

In 1990, the LOA heralded the Peace Atlantis I procurement

PORTUGUESE F-16
A Portuguese Air Force General Dynamics F-16BM takes off with afterburner prominent from Mont-de-Marsan airbase, France, during NATO exercises in 2019.

programme, which covered the first 20 Portuguese F-16s (17 F-16As and three F-16Bs) with Pratt & Whitney F100-PW-220E engines together with logistic support, spare parts, support equipment, technical manuals, and training for pilot and maintenance personnel. These initial aircraft were newly built Block 15OCU jets – broadly equivalent to the F-16 ADF variant for the US Air Force, including AIM-7 Sparrow missile capability.

Specific changes for Portuguese service included Advanced Identification Friend or Foe (AIFF) – identified by the 'bird slicer' antennas ahead of the cockpit canopy – an identification light on the port side of the nose and the bulges at the base of the tailfin housing the actuators for the stabilators. An acceptance ceremony for the first two Portuguese F-16s took place in February 1994, and the first four were delivered in July of the same year.

The next batch of Portuguese F-16s was acquired under Peace Atlantis II in 1996. This time,

second-hand Block 15 aircraft were involved in the form of 25 former US Air Force jets (21 F-16As and four F-16Bs). These aircraft were primarily intended to replace A-7Ps in the ground-attack role, although before long they were also being used for air defence missions.

The Peace Atlantis II jets were transferred to Portugal as Excess Defence Articles, and at no charge, with the required modifications being undertaken in Portugal prior to service entry. However, five of the aircraft did not enter squadron service, instead being used as sources of spare parts.

In the meantime, Portugal had already signed up for the MLU programme for its existing Peace Atlantis I jets.

The modifications for all these aircraft included the Falcon UP structural upgrade, the F100-PW-220E engine upgrade and the MLU avionics and cockpit package. In addition, the upgraded aircraft

received a night identification light, a dedicated electronic warfare data bus, additional chaff/flare dispensers, and provision for an internal missile warning system.

As well as contributing to the NATO Baltic Air Policing mission, Portuguese F-16s have seen combat. In 1999, during Operation Allied Force over the former Yugoslavia, the jets were deployed to Aviano Air Base in Italy, from which they primarily flew combat air patrols.

Transfers of former Portuguese F-16s allowed Romania to establish its own Viper force. In total, Romania took 17 second-hand jets from Portuguese stocks in two batches between 2016 and 2020.

Poland

Poland occupies an exclusive position as the first former Warsaw Pact nation to order the F-16. Poland acquired 48 F-16C/D Block 52 jets under the Peace Sky programme. These were delivered

F-16D Block 52

Weight (maximum take-off): 19186.96kg (42,300lbs)

Dimensions: Length 15.06m (49ft 5in), Wingspan 9.448m (31ft), Height 5.09m (16ft 8in)

Powerplant: One Pratt & Whitney F100-PW-229 turbofan

Maximum speed: Mach 2.05

Range: 579km (360 miles)

Ceiling: 16,764m (55,000ft)

Crew: 2

Armament: One 20mm (0.787in) M61A1 six-barrel rotary cannon, plus six hardpoints

POLISH F-16D BLOCK 52
A Polish Air Force Lockheed Martin F-16D Block 52, 4076, serial number
03-0076, serving with 31st Tactical Air Base circa 2019.

POLISH F-16D
The trademark bubble canopy is prominent on this Polish Air Force F-16D at Leeuwarden, Netherlands, during NATO exercises in 2016.

between 2006 and 2008, making them some of the youngest – and most capable – F-16s available to NATO in Europe. After examining the Dassault Mirage 2000 and Saab Gripen, the Polish Air Force formally selected a US-made type as its new fighter in 1998, when it requested the government in Warsaw approve the lease of up to 36 aircraft. The new aircraft were primarily required to replace ageing Soviet-era jets still in Polish Air Force service, including the MiG-21 and Su-22.

Initially, the United States offered to lease second-hand F-16s or F/A-18s, over a five-year period. Eventually, however, Poland chose to buy 48 F-16s (comprising 36 single-seat F-16Cs and 12 two-seat F-16Ds). This type was confirmed by the Polish government in December 2002. The procurement programme was named Peace Sky and included offset agreements with Lockheed Martin that would see investment in Polish industry.

Finally, the Peace Sky contract was signed in April 2003, valued at $3.5 billion. As well as the 36 jets, this included spare F100-PW-229 engines, armament, technical manuals and training for Polish pilots. A first Polish F-16 made its maiden flight at Fort Worth on 14 March 2006.

With avionics based around the APG-68(V)9 radar, the Polish F-16s are equipped to a notably high standard. They are fitted with the AN/ALQ-211(V)4 electronic warfare suite and can be configured with Conformal Fuel Tanks. Polish F-16s are armed with AIM-120C-5/7 AMRAAMs and AIM-9X Sidewinder missiles that can be fired off-boresight using the Joint Helmet Mounted Cueing System (JHMCS). Offensive stores include the AGM-65 Maverick missile, the AGM-154 Joint Standoff Weapon (JSOW) and the AGM-158A/B Joint Air-to-Surface Standoff Missile (JASSM), as well as Paveway laser-guided bombs and Joint Direct Attack Munitions (JDAM). The aircraft are fitted with Sniper Extended Range targeting pods and can carry the Goodrich Corporation DB-110 tactical reconnaissance pod.

In a reconnaissance role, Polish F-16s were deployed to the Middle East to join the coalition force supporting Operation Inherent Resolve in the fight against the so-called Islamic State.

BULGARIAN COMMITMENT

In July 2019, the Bulgarian government announced the decision to buy new F-16C/D Block 70 jets to replace the ageing MiG-29 fighter fleet. The initial contract covers eight Block 70 aircraft (four F-16Cs and two F-16Ds) at a cost of $1.3 billion. Subsequently, Bulgaria exercised an option to buy a second batch of eight new F-16s. Deliveries were originally planned to begin in late 2023 but were delayed by the COVID-19 pandemic.

African and Middle Eastern Operators

The first of the F-16 customers in the Gulf region, Bahrain selected the aircraft as part of a modernisation programme for the Royal Bahraini Air Force (RBAD) launched in the late 1980s. After acquiring 22 F-16C/D Block 40 aircraft in two batches, Bahrain subsequently placed orders for 16 of the latest-production Block 70 version, from the new production line at Greenville in South Carolina. The first Block 70 aircraft to be formally rolled out, a two-seat F-16D model, in March 2023, was also the first of the new batch for the RBAF.

EMIRATI-F-16
A United Arab Emirates Air Force (UAEAF)
F-16 disconnects from a US Air Force
KC-10A Extender after refueling during
a multinational exercise.

F-16DG Block 40
Night Falcon
Weight (maximum take-off): 19,187kg (42,300lbs)
Dimensions: Length
15.04m (49ft 4in); Wingspan
9.4488m (31ft); Height
5.09m (16ft 8.5in)
Powerplant: One General
Electric F110-GE-100
turbofan
Maximum speed:
Mach 2.02
Range: 579km (360 miles)
Ceiling: 16,764m (55,000ft)
Crew: 2
Armament: One 20mm
(0.787in) M61A1 six-barrel
rotary cannon, plus six
hardpoints

**BAHRAINI F-16DG BLOCK 40
NIGHT FALCON**
This Royal Bahraini Air Force (RBAD)
General Dynamics F-16DG Block 40
Night Falcon, serial number 90-0039,
dates from circa 2008.

Bahrain
The first F-16 order for the RBAF
was covered by the Peace Crown I
Foreign Military Sales programme,
which a Letter of Agreement was
signed in March 1987, comprising
12 Block 40 aircraft (eight F-16Cs
and four F-16Ds). The first of these,
a two-seater, was formally handed
over at Fort Worth in March
1989. The first four aircraft were
delivered to Bahrain in May 1990,
shortly before the Iraqi invasion of
Kuwait. The RBAF F-16s would fly
defensive and offensive missions
during the 1991 Gulf War.

In February 1998, a Letter of
Offer and Acceptance was signed
to launch Peace Crown II, which
provided the RBAF with a second
batch of new-build F-16s. Valued
at $303 million, it comprised
10 more Block 40 jets, this time
all single-seaters. The new jets

had LANTIRN and AMRAAM
capability; previously, their
beyond-visual-range armament
had been limited to the AM-7
Sparrow. In June 2018, Lockheed
Martin was awarded a $1.12-billion
contract to provide Bahrain with
new Block 70 aircraft, to equip
a new squadron. The 16 aircraft
will comprise 10 single-seat
F-16Cs and six dual-seat variants.
Deliveries are planned from 2024.
Together with the new Block 70
jets, Bahrain has elected to upgrade
the surviving Block 40 airframes
to a similar standard, including
the AN/APG-83 AESA radar and
advanced avionics.

Egypt
Having received a total of 220
F-16s, the Egyptian Air Force
(EAF) is the fourth-largest Viper
operator in the world. Although
orders and deliveries have, at
time, been interrupted by political
considerations, the F-16 remains
the most important combat aircraft
type in the EAF inventory, serving
in a varied fleet alongside MiG-29s
and Rafales.

F-16A Block 15H

Weight (maximum take-off): 17,010kg (37,500lbs)

Dimensions: Length 15.01m (49ft 3.5in); Wing-span 9.995m (32ft 9.5in); Height 5.09m (16ft 8.5in)

Powerplant: One Pratt & Whitney F100-PW-220 turbofan

Maximum speed: Mach 2.05 at 40,000ft

Range: 3862km (2400 miles)

Ceiling: 16,764m (55,000ft)

Crew: 1

Armament: One 20mm (0.787in) M61A1 six-barrel rotary cannon, plus six hardpoints

Egypt's path to becoming an F-16 customer started with the signing of a peace agreement with Israel in 1979. This meant that the country was now able to procure advanced weapons systems from the United States.

The first F-16 deal for Egypt was Peace Vector I, for which a letter of agreement was signed in June 1980. This Foreign Military Sales contract covered 42 F-16A/B

EGYPTIAN F-16A BLOCK 15H
An Egyptian Air Force General Dynamics F-16A Block 15H, 9324, serial number 81-0661, serving with 232 Tactical Fighter Wing.

EGYPTIAN F-16B BLOCK 15H
An Egyptian Air Force General Dynamics F-16B Block 15H, 9822, serial number 10-1018, serving with 292 Tactical Fighter Wing.

Block 15 aircraft, comprising 34 single-seaters and eight two-seaters. The first F-16 for the EAF was accepted during a ceremony at Fort Worth in January 1982 and the first aircraft were delivered to Egypt the following March. By the mid-1990s, work was underway to upgrade the Block 15 aircraft to the more capable Block 42 standard. The modernisation programme included most Block 40/42

features, although the aircraft retained the Pratt & Whitney F100 with the smaller engine intake.

Peace Vector II, the next Egyptian F-16 order, provided the EAF with 40 F-16C/D Block 32 versions (34 single-seaters and six two-seaters). With Washington unwilling to approve the sale of AMRAAM missiles, these aircraft were instead provided with the AIM-7 Sparrow. The first of the Peace Vector II aircraft arrived in Egypt in October 1986. In common with the earlier Block 15s, these aircraft were also later modernised to Block 42 standard.

In June 1990, Egypt signed its third Viper order, with the Peace Vector III contract covering 47

Block 40 aircraft (35 F-16Cs and 12 F-16Ds), powered by the F110 turbofan. Deliveries to Egypt began in October 1991.

Unlike the EAF's previous F-16 batches, the Peace Vector IV aircraft were assembled under licence by Turkish Aerospace Industries (TAI). This contract was for 46 more Block 40 aircraft, in the form of 34 F-16Cs and 12 F-16Ds. This was the first time that F-16s built outside of the United States had been sold to a third-party nation. Deliveries to Egypt took place between 1994 and 1995.

Signed in May 1996, Peace Vector V provided the EAF with another batch of 21 F-16C/D Block 40 aircraft powered by

F110 engines. Once again, these jets came from the Fort Worth production facility, where the first aircraft rolled off the line in 1999.

In March 1999, Egypt and the United States agreed a major new arms deal, which included 24 more F-16 Block 40 aircraft under Peace Vector VI. The aircraft were supplied in the form of 12 F-16Cs and 12 F-16Ds and the sixth batch also came equipped with AGM-88 HARM missiles for the defence suppression mission.

The more recent batch of Egyptian F-16 deliveries were provided under Peace Vector VII, with a contract signed in December 2009. This covered the supply of 20 Pratt & Whitney-

---

F-16D Block 52

Weight (maximum take-off): 19,187kg (42,300lb)

Dimensions: Length 15.06m (49ft 5in), Wingspan 9.96m (32ft 8in), Height 4.9m (16ft)

Powerplant: One Pratt & Whitney F100-PW-229 turbofan

Maximum speed: Mach 2.05

Range: 4217km (2620 miles), with drop tanks

Ceiling: 16,764m (55,000ft)

Crew: 2

Armament: One 20mm (0.787in) M61A1 six-barrel rotary cannon, plus up to 7700kg (17,000lb) of disposable stores carried on six underwing, two wingtip and one centreline hardpoint

IRAQI AIR FORCE F-16D BLOCK 52
This Lockheed Martin F-16D Block 52, 1602, serial number 12-0017, serves with the 9th Fighter Squadron of the Iraqi Air Force, based at Balad Airport, Salahuddin Province.

engined F-16s, which were also the first Block 52s for Egypt. Sixteen of the jets were single-seat F-16Cs, with four two-seat F-16Ds.

Iraq

Following the 2003 US-led invasion and the long-running insurgency that followed, the Iraqi Air Force was entirely rebuilt, with the F-16 being acquired as its most capable combat aircraft. While these aircraft have seen considerable combat action against forces of so-called Islamic State, the Iraqi Viper fleet has suffered from poor serviceability. In all, 36 F-16 Block 52 aircraft were delivered to Baghdad, in two batches. Iraq first expressed

an interest in acquiring F-16s in September 2008, with the aim of increasingly taking on responsibility for air combat missions as the US mission in the country started to wind down. The first Iraqi F-16 order was announced In 2011 and covered 18 aircraft: 12 F-16C and six F-16Ds.

In October 2012 a follow-on buy was confirmed, providing Iraq with another 18 F-16s. This time, 16 of the jets were F-16Cs, with two F-16Ds.

Iraqi F-16s, despite their advanced avionics and configuration, were not supplied with the more sensitive AIM-120 AMRAAM missiles and instead rely on the older AM-7 Sparrow.

Other equipment supplied includes DB-110 reconnaissance pods.

Israel

One of the world's most capable and combat-proven air arms, the Israeli Air Force (IAF) has long been an enthusiastic operator of the F-16, with a total of 362 examples ordered through the years. The recent arrival of the F-35 – known locally as the Adir ('Mighty', in Hebrew) – has seen the earlier F-16A/B models retired from service after decades of heavy use, although the more modern variants, including the Israel-specific F-16I Sufa (Storm), continue to provide the backbone of the combat fleet, well equipped

as they are with locally developed avionics and weapons.

Israel began to show interest in the F-16 even before it had entered US Air Force service. Plans to acquire the F-16A/B were announced by Israel in August 1978. Despite a more restrictive US arms sales policy introduced under the administration of President Jimmy Carter, Washington approved the deal. The Peace Marble I contract comprised 75 Block 5 and 10 aircraft, with the earlier versions brought up to the latter standard before delivery. The aircraft consisted of 67 F-16As and eight F-16Bs, which, ironically, had originally been intended for delivery to Iran – one of Israel's major adversaries in the region.

The first four IAF F-16s arrived in Israel in July 1980. Israel's raid on the Osirak nuclear reactor in Iraq (a mission that involved F-16s) led to a suspension of deliveries, but the last Peace Marble I aircraft were transferred in 1981.

The Israeli F-16A/B, known locally as Netz ('Sparrowhawk'), introduced a number of specific modifications, kicking off a process in which these jets incorporated a growing proportion of domestically produced systems and weapons. The Israeli F-16A/B had changes made to its mission computers, for example, allowing the use of locally made weapons, while indigenous electronic warfare systems were also added, including electronic

countermeasures in the fin-root fairing. From the early 1990s, the surviving Peace Marble I aircraft were upgraded by Israel Aircraft Industries (IAI), emerging with structural reinforcements to the wings and a new flight and mission management system from IAI's Elbit subsidiary. Once complete, these aircraft were broadly the same standard as the F-16C/D, although they retained the F100 engine.

Israeli F-16C/D

Israel began to receive the new F-16C/D Block 30 versions under Peace Marble II, with deliveries commencing in October 1987. A total of 75 Block 30 aircraft were delivered: 51 F-16Cs and 24 F-16Ds. These aircraft are known as Barak (Lightning).

The Israeli F-16C/D also features some specific differences, including an extension at the base of the tail fin, accommodating additional defensive avionics fits. To operate at higher gross weights, the undercarriage was also beefed up. Later F-16C/Ds were fitted with Elta EL/L-8240 electronic countermeasures (ECM) internally as part of an indigenous electronic warfare self-protection suite.

The two-seat F-16D Barak was optimized for combat missions, rather than training, with a weapons system operator in the rear cockpit. The aircraft also introduced a prominent dorsal extension running from the rear of the cockpit to the vertical stabilizer. The dorsal spine is primarily

used to house additional avionics, including elements of the electronic warfare self-protection suite, likely including a self-protection jammer.

After Israel abandoned plans to develop the indigenous Lavi fighter jet in 1988, the country turned again to the United States for more F-16s. The Peace Marble III order consisted of 60 Block 40 aircraft, in the form of 30 F-16Cs and 30 F-16Ds, plus an option for 15 more. The first of these F-16s were delivered to Israel in August 1991.

In the meantime, the 1991 Gulf War had led to some significant changes in the security situation in the Middle East, with Israel having come under attack from Iraqi Scud missiles. Despite the missile raids, Israel did not retaliate, and this was rewarded by the United States providing the IAF with 50 second-hand US Air Force F-16A/B Block 10 aircraft, known as Netz 2. The first of these, under the Peace Marble IV programme, was delivered in August 1994, and the last had been handed over before the end of that year.

With the Peace Marble V programme, the IAF received a bespoke version of the F-16 tailored to its needs. The decision to acquire a new type of fighter jet was announced by the Israeli Ministry of Defence in mid-1997, with either more F-16s or F-15I Ra'am aircraft being anticipated. The IAF, meanwhile, outlined a requirement for between 50 and 100 new fighters to replace ageing Douglas A-4 Skyhawks, McDonnell Douglas F-4 Phantom IIs and older

F-16C BLOCK 40G
Weight (maximum load):
21,772kg (48,000lbs)
Dimensions: Length
15.02m (49ft 3in); Wingspan
9.4488m (31ft 3in); Height
5.09m (16ft 7in)
Powerplant: One Pratt
and Whitney F100-
PW-200/220/229 or General
Electric F110-GE-100/129
Maximum Speed: Mach
2.02 at 40,000ft
Range: Maximum ferry
range with external fuel:
3218km (2000 miles)
Ceiling: 18,000m (60,000ft)
Crew: 2
Armament: One 20mm
(0.787in) M61A1 six-barrel
rotary cannon, plus up to
7700kg (17,000lb) of
disposable stores carried
on six underwing, two
wingtip and one centreline
hardpoint

ISRAELI F-16D BLOCK 40
This F-16D Block 40 Fighting Falcon
served with 150 "Scorpion" Squadron,
based at Hatzor Air Force Base in
central Israel. Known as the Brakeet
II ("Thunderbolt"), this version was
delivered in 1991. It is armed
with a GBU-15 glide bomb on
the starboard outer wing, with a
Mk 82 227kg (500lb) bomb for
balance on the port side.

ISRAELI F-16I TEST FLIGHT

ISRAELI F-16I TEST FLIGHT
Israeli Air Force F-16Is from Ramon
Air Base, Israel, head out to the
Nevada Test and Training Range,
Nevada, United States, during Red
Flag 09-4, c. 2009. Red Flag is a
realistic combat training exercise
involving the air forces of the United
States and its allies.

F-16s. The service also noted that
long range and a significant degree
of sophistication were to be prized.

In September 1998, the US
government made two offers to
Israel: either 30 more F-15Is or
60 F-16C/D. In each case, the
deal would be worth around $2.5
billion. In early 1999, Israel said
it would now be looking to spend
as much as $4 billion on the order
– equivalent to around 110 F-16s.
The possibility of a split F-15/F-16
deal was also raised.

F-16I *Sufa*

In the meantime, Lockheed Martin
campaigned hard to defeat the
F-15I, offering a two-seat strike-
optimized version of the F-16 that
would have extended range thanks
to conformal fuel tanks (CFTs).

Finally, in January 2000, the
Israeli government announced
it would buy 50 F-16D Block
52-equivalent aircraft, with specific
Israeli modifications, known locally
as F-16I *Sufa*. The deal was valued
at approximately $2.5 billion,
with an option to buy 60 more. In
September 2001, an option for 52
more F-16I aircraft was exercised,
for a total of 102 aircraft valued at
around $4.5 billion.

The roll-out ceremony for the
F-16I took place at Fort Worth
in November 2003, involving the
fourth production aircraft. The first
pair of F-16Is were delivered to
Israel in February 2004.

IAF F-16s of all variants use
a wide variety of indigenous
weaponry, including infrared-
guided Python 4 and 5 air-to-air
missiles and Popeye and Spice
standoff air-to-ground missiles.

Combat record

The combat record of the IAF F-16
fleet is second to none, with official
claims of 47 air-to-air kills since
the type's combat debut in Israeli
hands in April 1981 when a Netz
shot down a Syrian Mi-8 helicopter
over Lebanon. According to Israeli
accounts, during the combat
over Lebanon's Bekaa Valley that
followed in 1982, the IAF's F-16s
achieved a 44-0 kill ratio.

The F-16 has been at the
forefront of Israeli military
campaigns since then, with more
recent operations including
participation in the 2006 Ebb
and Flow and 2008–09 Cast Lead

operations in Gaza, along with the Second Lebanon War in July 2006.

Jordan

The Royal Jordanian Air Force (RJAF) is a long-term Viper operator, having acquired ex-US Air Force airframes as well as former Belgian and Dutch aircraft. It has taken its F-16s into combat as part of the coalition fighting the so-called Islamic State.

F-16AM Fighting Falcon
Weight (maximum take-off): 17,010kg (37,500lbs)
Dimensions: Length 15.01m (49ft 3.5in); Wing-span 9.995m (32ft 9.5in); Height 5.09m (16ft 8.5in)
Powerplant: One Pratt & Whitney F100-PW-220 turbofan
Maximum speed: Mach 2.05 at 40,000ft
Range: 3862km (2400 miles)
Ceiling: 16,764m (55,000ft)
Crew: 1
Armament: One 20mm (0.787in) M61A1 six-barrel rotary cannon, plus six hardpoints

The RJAF's first batch of F-16s was acquired under the Peace Falcon I deal signed in July 1996. Valued at $220 million, this deal initially involved the lease of 16 Block 15 aircraft (12 single-seat F-16As and four two-seat F-16Bs). Also included were structural upgrades under the Falcon Up/Service Life Improvement programme, modifications that added the F100-220E engine, support equipment, spare parts and pilot and maintainer training. The aircraft themselves were former Block 15 OCU jets that went through modifications that brought them up to ADF standard. The aircraft had seen previous service with the active US Air Force and Air National Guard before being stored at the Aerospace Maintenance and Regeneration Center (AMARC) at Davis Monthan Air Force Base in Arizona.

The first of the refurbished F-16s for the RJAF took to the air after modifications at Hill Air Force Base, Utah, in October 1997. An official rollout for the first

Peace Falcon I jet took place in the same month.

Peace Falcon II provided the RJAF with another batch of former US Air National Guard Block 15 ADF aircraft – 17 in all, made up of 16 F-16As and one F-16B. However, most of these jets, delivered in 2003, were initially placed in storage pending modernization to MLU standards, a process carried out by Turkish Aerospace Industries (TAI) in Ankara. The aircraft were then inducted into RJAF service before the end of that decade.

To further boost F-16 numbers within the RJAF, in 2006, Amman secured the Peace Falcon III deal with the Belgian and Dutch governments. In total, this package was intended to provide 22 aircraft: eight former Royal Netherlands Air Force (five F-16As and three F-16Bs) and 14 ex-Belgian Air Force (12 F-16As and two F-16Bs). All these aircraft would go undergo the MLU upgrade prior to delivery to Jordan.

In 2009, 16 ex-Belgian F-16s (12 F-16As and four F-16Bs) were

JORDANIAN F-16AM
A General Dynamics (SABCA) F-16AM
Fighting Falcon (401) from the Royal
Jordanian Air Force.

MOROCCAN F-16D BLOCK 52

This Lockheed Martin F-16D Block 52, serial number 08-8020, served with
the Esc de Chasse, Royal Moroccan Air Force, circa 2011.

F-16D Block 52

**Weight (maximum take-
off):** 19,187kg (42,300lb)

Dimensions: Length
15.06m (49ft 5in), Wingspan
9.96m (32ft 8in), Height
4.9m (16ft)

Powerplant: One Pratt
& Whitney F100-PW-229
turbofan

Maximum speed:
Mach 2.05

Range: 4217km (2620
miles), with drop tanks

Ceiling: 16,764m (55,000ft)

Crew: 2

Armament: One 20mm
(0.787in) M61A1 six-barrel
rotary cannon, plus up to
7700kg (17,000lb) of
disposable stores carried
on six underwing, two
wingtip and one centreline
hardpoint

delivered, but the Dutch F-16As
were ultimately not included in
Peace Falcon III.

Instead, Peace Falcon IV
provided Jordan with six former
RNLAF F-16Bs, which were also
handed over in 2009. Meanwhile,
Peace Falcon V covered another
batch of former Belgian jets: six
F-16As and three F-16Bs, all of
which were delivered in 2011.

The latest Jordanian contract,
Peace Falcon VI, was announced
by the Dutch government in 2012,
covering 15 more airframes
(13 F-16As and two F-16Bs).
Deliveries were delayed but finally
took place in 2017.

Morocco

To provide a boost to its combat
fleet, which comprised Northrop
F-5E/F Tiger IIs and Dassault
Mirage F1s, the Royal Moroccan
Air Force (RMAF) received 24
F-16C/Ds, all new-build jets from
the Block 52 production batch. In
particular, the new fighters were
acquired in response to Algeria's
purchase of MiG-29SMT and
Su-30MKA aircraft from Russia.
Morocco placed its order for

Vipers in 2008, choosing the F-16
in preference to the Rafale. The
total cost of the Moroccan deal was
placed at $2.4 billion. Deliveries
took place between 2010 and 2011.

Oman

Oman received 24 F-16C/Ds – all
new-build examples from the
Block 50 production batch. These
aircraft are notably well-equipped.
As well as AN/APG-68(V)XM and
Sniper navigation and targeting
pods (late-supplemented by the
more advanced Pantera pods), the
Omani jets feature some highly
capable weapons options, including
AIM-120 AMRAAM air-to-air
missiles, AGM-65 air-to-ground
missiles, AGM-84 Harpoon
anti-ship missiles, GBU-10 and
GBU-12 laser-guided bombs, Joint
Direct Attack Munition (JDAM)
precision-guided bombs and CBU-
97/105 Sensor Fuzed Weapons.
DB-110 reconnaissance pods were
also provided.

The first Omani Viper
contract was secured after the
US government approved a
$1.1-billion transfer of 12 F-16C/
Ds in October 2001. Also included

in the package were weapons, equipment and technical and logistical support. A corresponding agreement was signed in May 2002 under the Peace A'sama A'safiya I (Clear Skies) programme. This Foreign Military Sales deal included eight single-seat F-16Cs and four two-seat F-16Ds powered by F110-GE-129 engines.

The first F-16 for the Royal Air Force of Oman (RAFO) was accepted at Fort Worth in August 2005. The first two aircraft were delivered to Oman in October of the same year, with the remainder following in 2006. The second batch of RAFO F-16s, to the same standard as the previous ones, was secured under Peace A'sama A'safiya II, announced in August 2010. This contract also covered 12 aircraft, but this time comprising 10 F-16Cs and two F-16Ds. Deliveries took place in 2014.

United Arab Emirates

The United Arab Emirates (UAE) is unique in operating the F-16E/F Block 60 aircraft, named Desert Falcon. At the time the order was placed, the Block 60 was the most advanced F-16 version available, and the 80 aircraft were provided together with sophisticated weapons including AIM-120 AMRAAM air-to-air missiles, AGM-65 air-to-ground missiles, AGM-84 Harpoon anti-ship missiles, AGM-88 HARM anti-radiation missiles and laser-guided bombs. The UAE began to look seriously at buying F-16s in September 1996 when the government announced that this aircraft, together with the Dassault Rafale, were the final candidates in a competitive process to buy a new fighter aircraft. To ensure it secured the contract, Lockheed Martin offered the UAE

the highly advanced Block 60 configuration, with conformal fuel tanks (CFTs) and an internally mounted forward-looking infrared (FLIR) sensor. In May 1998, the UAE government announced the selection of the Block 60 as its new fighter. The 80 aircraft were to be acquired in the form of 55 single-seat F-16Cs and 25 two-seat F-16Ds. The total package was worth around $7 billion.

The first F-16 Block 60 for the UAE made its maiden flight on 6 December 2003 at Fort Worth, with Lockheed Martin test pilot Steve Barter at the controls. Deliveries took place between 2004 and 2006.

UAE F-16E

An F-16E from Al Dhafra Air Base, United Arab Emirates, takes off for a training exercise over the Nevada Test and Training Range, United States.

TRAINING MISSION
A United Arab Emirates Air Force (UAEAF) F-16E from the 162nd Fighter
Wing manoeuvres during a training mission out of Tucson International
Airport, Arizona.

Asia-Pacific Operators

The F-16 is the most numerous fighter jet in the inventory of the South Korean air arm – the Republic of Korea Air Force (ROKAF) – with a total of 180 F-16C/D aircraft having been acquired in both Block 30 and Block 52 versions. South Korea also locally assembled some of these aircraft, which are alternatively known as KF-16s.

PAKISTANI F-16

A Pakistan Air Force Lockheed Martin F-16 takes off from Izmir, Turkey, during joint exercises, 2011.

SOUTH KOREAN F-16A FIGHTING FALCON
The 8th Tactical Fighter Wing based at Kunsan in Korea was the first unit
outside the United States to be equipped with F-16s, when it exchanged its last
F-4 Phantoms for the new type in May 1981. This Fighting Falcon wears the
codes and emblem of the 8th TFW, known as the 'Wolf Pack'.

After first looking at a purchase of
as many as 72 F-16s in the mid-
1970s, the United States proposed a
deal for 60 of the F-16A/Bs in 1978,
before switching to the export-
optimized F-16/79. In the event,
however, when South Korea signed
a letter of agreement for the Peace
Bridge I deal in December 1981,
this covered 36 F-16C/D Block 32
aircraft (30 F-16Cs and six F-16Ds)
procured through Foreign Military
Sales channels. These were the
first F-16C/Ds to be approved for
export anywhere in the world.
An official handover ceremony
for the first two ROKAF F-16Ds
took place at Daegu Air Base in
April 1986. In June 1988, Peace
Bridge I eventually added another
four F-16D Block 32s, providing a
total of 40 aircraft in this deal: 30
single-seat F-16Cs and 10 two-seat
F-16Ds. These last two-seaters
were delivered in 1992.

After assessing the F/A-18
Hornet as part of the Korean

Fighter Program (KFP)
competition, Seoul then signed a
deal for more F-16s, under Peace
Bridge II. This deal covered 120
F-16s (80 F-16Cs and 40 F-16Ds)
that would be completed to Block
52 standard, with upgraded
avionics and F100-PW-229
engines. Lockheed Martin
produced the first 12 aircraft only,
after which manufacture was
handled in South Korea.

For the next 36 aircraft,
Samsung Aerospace would receive
knock-down kits from Lockheed;
the remaining 72 jets would be
produced entirely in South Korea.
These locally assembled aircraft are
also known as KF-16C/Ds.

The first (Lockheed-built)
F-16 from Peace Bridge II was
formally delivered to South Korea
in December 1994. Meanwhile,
in June 1997, the first Korean-
assembled KF-16 was handed over
at the Samsung Aerospace facility
in Sachon.

F-16A FIGHTING FALCON
**Weight (maximum take-
off):** 17,009.71kg (37,500lbs)
Dimensions: Length
15.01m (49ft 3.5in); Wing-
span 9.995m (32ft 9.5in);
Height 5.09m (16ft 8.5in)
Powerplant: One Pratt
& Whitney F100-PW-220
turbofan
Maximum speed: Mach
2.05 at 40,000ft
Range: 3862km
(2400 miles)
Ceiling: 16,764m (55,000ft)
Crew: 1
Armament: One M61A1
20mm (0.787in) cannon
(500 rd); six hardpoints:
AIM-9 Sidewinder, AIM-7
Sparrow, AIM-120 AMRAAM
air-to-air missiles

Seoul's most recent order for new-build F-16s was Peace Bridge III, signed with the US government in July 2000. This deal covered another 20 F-16C/D Block 52s, consisting of 15 F-16Cs and five F-16Ds. These aircraft were assembled locally by Korean Aerospace Industries (KAI) and delivered between 2003 and 2004. These additional jets allowed the continued replacement of the F-5E/F Tiger II.

New equipment

The ROKAF's advanced Block 52 jets are equipped with the LANTIRN navigation and targeting pod and can be armed with AIM-120 AMRAAM air-to-air missiles and AGM-88 HARM anti-radiation missiles. The South Korean jets were also the first export examples to feature the AN/ALQ-165 Airborne Self-Protection Jammer (ASPJ). This internal electronic countermeasures suite was retrofitted in ROKAF Block 52 F-16s, and a first modified

example was delivered in February 1999. The ROKAF jets can also be configured for tactical reconnaissance, using pods of Israeli and Korean manufacture, for which the semi-official designation RKF-16C is applied.

Under Peace Bridge, the ROKAF undertook upgrades of its 35 surviving F-16C/D Block 32 aircraft, including by adding an Improved Data Modem and secure voice capabilities, together with the GBU-31 Joint Direct Attack Munition (JDAM) and AMRAAM. Work was completed in 2016. A further upgrade for the Block 32 fleet added Mode 5 identification friend or foe (IFF) and the Link 16 tactical datalink.

Upgrade programme

An upgrade programme is now underway for the ROKAF's F-16C/D Block 52 fleet, around 130 of which (minus attrition losses) are being brought up to F-16V standard at a cost of around $1.2 billion, after an earlier deal

F-16CJ BLOCK 52

Weight (maximum take-off): 19,187kg (42,300lb)

Dimensions: Length 15.06m (49ft 5in), Wingspan 9.96m (32ft 8in), Height 4.9m (16ft)

Powerplant: One General Electric F110-GE-129 turbofan

Maximum speed: Mach 2.05

Range: 4217km (2620 miles), with drop tanks

Ceiling: 18,288m (60,000ft)

Crew: 1

Armament: One 20mm (0.787in) M61A1 six-barrel rotary cannon, plus up to 7700kg (17,000lb) of disposable stores carried on six hardpoints, including AGM-88 High-speed Anti-Radiation Missile (HARM) and AGM-45 Shrike anti-radiation missiles

SOUTH KOREAN F-16CJ
A Samsung F-16C Block 52D, 93-065 (serial number 93-4065), 19th Fighter Wing, Republic of Korea Air Force.

An Indonesian Air Force F-16AM Fighting Falcon sits in an airfield near Jakarta, Java, April 2021.

between the ROKAF and BAE Systems fell through.

This modernization features the Northrop Grumman AN/APG-83 Scalable Agile Beam Radar (SABR), the Joint Helmet Mounted Cueing System II (JHMCS II) and improved cockpit displays and mission computers. For self-protection, the upgraded jet is equipped with the BAE Systems AN/ALR-56M Advanced Radar Warning Receiver.

The first two aircraft, a KF-16C and KF-16D, were upgraded at the Fort Worth facility, and the single-seater made its first flight after modification in August 2019. The upgrade work is expected to be completed by around 2025.

Indonesia

Today, the F-16 is an important part of a diverse Indonesian Air Force fighter fleet, with the Viper component comprising around eight survivors from the original 12 F-16A/B Block 15 OCU fighters delivered from 1989, plus 23 upgraded former US Air Force F-16C/Ds from an original total of 24.

Jakarta's process of acquiring F-16s has not always been easy, however, with a US arms embargo in place between 1999 and 2005. This embargo was a result of human rights violations in East Timor, which held up deliveries.

Under the Peace Bima-Sena I, the Indonesian Air Force received its first Vipers, with a letter of agreement for 12 F-16A/B Block 15 OCU aircraft signed in August 1986. The first Indonesian F-16 was delivered in December 1989, and the last, in 1990.

In 1996, Jakarta planned a follow-on order for an additional nine F-16A Block 15 fighters, and a contract was signed with the manufacturer. These aircraft were planned to be diverted from a cancelled Pakistani order. A year later, however, Indonesia also cancelled its order, turning instead to Moscow for new fighter jets. Despite the introduction of the

Sukhoi Su-27 and Su-30 Flanker, Indonesia's F-16 purchases did not come to an end. With the $750 million Peace Bima-Sena II programme announced in 2011, Indonesia received a total of 24 ex-US Air Force F-16C/D Block 25 aircraft, all of which were refurbished before delivery and brought up to Block 50/52 standards. Another six Block 15 and 25 airframes were also included in the deal as a spare parts source. Deliveries of the Peace Bima-Sena II jets took place between 2015 and 2017. Efforts were also made to bring the surviving Indonesian F-16A/B fleet up to a similar standard via the MLU upgrade to increase commonality across the fleet.

Pakistan

Despite the introduction of the Chinese-made Chengdu J-10, as well as the JF-17 Thunder (jointly developed by Pakistan and China), the F-16 remains the major fighter jet in the Pakistan Air Force (PAF). These aircraft were acquired from the United States in several batches beginning in the 1980s, although deliveries were interrupted by an arms embargo in response to Pakistan's nuclear weapons programme. Since then, advanced F-16C/D Block 52 jets have been delivered bringing new capabilities in the process.

The first Vipers for the PAF were procured under the Peace Gate I and II contracts, with a letter of agreement signed in December 1981 covering the purchase of 40 F-16A/B Block 15 aircraft (28 F-16As and 12 F-16Bs) powered by F100-PW-200 engines. The contract covered two batches: the first, six aircraft, and the second, 34. The first aircraft – from Peace Gate I – were accepted at Fort Worth in October 1982, and for the PAF, the first F-16 arrived in Pakistan in January 1983. The six Peace Gate I aircraft consisted of two F-16As and four F-16Bs. The

F16DJ BLOCK 52
Weight (maximum take-off): 19,187kg (42,300lbs)
Dimensions: Length 15.06m (49ft 5in), Wingspan 9.448m (31ft), Height 5.09m (16ft 8in)
Powerplant: One Pratt & Whitney F100-PW-229 turbofan
Maximum speed: Mach 2.05
Range: 579km (360 miles)
Ceiling: 16,764m (55,000ft)
Crew: 2
Armament: One 20mm (0.787in) M61A1 six-barrel rotary cannon, plus up to 7700kg (17,000lb) of disposable stores carried on six hardpoints, including AGM-88 High-speed Anti-Radiation Missile (HARM) and AGM-45 Shrike anti-radiation missiles

PAKISTANI F-16DJ BLOCK 52
A Lockheed Martin F-16DJ Block 52, 10804 (serial number 07-0016),
5th Squadron, Pakistan Air Force, circa 2010.

remaining 34 aircraft were covered by Peace Gate II, deliveries of which were completed in 1987.

In December 1988, Pakistan ordered another 11 F-16A/B Block 15 OCU aircraft under Peace Gate III. These were divided as six F-16As and five F-16Bs acquired as attrition replacements to make good earlier losses with the Peace Gate I and II aircraft. However, with US concern about Pakistan's nuclear programme, the 11 aircraft were withheld and instead put into storage in the Aircraft Maintenance and Regeneration Center (AMARC) at Davis-Monthan Air Force Base, Arizona.

In September 1989, Pakistan announced plans to buy 60 more F-16A/Bs under the Peace Gate IV programme. A Foreign Military Sales contract was signed, valued at around $1.4 billion, and by the

end of 1994, 17 of these jets had been built. Like the 11 Peace Gate III aircraft, however, they were put into storage at AMARC, awaiting a lifting of the US arms embargo on Pakistan. Plans to sell nine of the Peace Gate III F-16s to Indonesia fell through, and a potential New Zealand order also came to nothing. Eventually, the 28 aircraft in storage (11 from Peace Gate III and the 17 completed under Peace Gate IV) were taken on strength by the US Air Force and Navy in 2002 as aggressor jets. The US Navy aircraft filled in a capability gap left by the previous retirement of the service's dedicated F-16N adversary aircraft.

'Peace Drive' delivery

Subsequent F-16 deliveries to Pakistan were covered by a new programme named Peace Drive and

involved more capable F-16C/D Block 52 aircraft. In March 2005, the US government announced it had agreed to supply Pakistan with 24 new-build F-16C/Ds as part of a wider package that also included MLU upgrades for its older F-16 A/B models.

In September 2006, a contract was signed for the sale of 18 new F-16C/Ds plus an option for 18 more. At the same time, it was agreed to finally deliver the 26 remaining Peace Gate III/IV aircraft that had been embargoes and to bring surviving F-16A/B aircraft to MLU standards.

JOINT EXERCISES
A Pakistan Air Force F-16 Fighting Falcon (85728) takes part in joint exercise Antatolian Eagle 2022 in Konya, Turkey.

PEACE OFFERING

The Royal Thai Air Force (RTAF) ordered a total of 54 F-16A/B aircraft that were delivered in four separate orders. Subsequently, it increased its fleet by acquiring seven more F-16A/Bs that were donated by Singapore.

Thailand first approached the United States with a view to buying F-16s in the mid-1980s, with the export-optimized F-16/79 version originally under consideration. In December 1987, the US and Thai governments signed the Peace Naresuan I Foreign Military Sales deal, which now included the F100-powered F-16. Initially, eight F-16As and four F-16Bs were procured, all Block 15 OCU jets, with deliveries taking place in 1988. Peace Naresuan II added six more F-16As for the RTAF. These were also Block 15 OCU jets and were delivered between 1990 and 1991. The very last Block 15 jets for any customer were included in Thailand's Peace Naresuan III order, which provided 18 more OCU jets: 12 F-16As and six F-16Bs. These were delivered between 1995 and 1996.

The last Thai F-16 order to be directly negotiated with the US government was Peace Naresuan IV, announced in July 2000, which provided another 16 F-16A/Bs (15 single-seaters and one two-seater), this time in the Block 15 ADF version. Instead of being new builds, these jets were provided to Thailand from US Air Force stocks and were delivered between 2002 and 2003.

In late 2013, it was announced that Pakistan was poised to bolster its F-16 fleet through the acquisition of a batch of second-hand aircraft from Jordan's Peace Falcon I contract. The 13 aircraft were provided in the form of nine F-16As and four F-16Bs which had not undergone the MLU upgrade, remaining in the ADF version. Deliveries took place in 2014.

Weapons stores

Pakistani F-16s have featured some unusual weapons and stores options through the years. With the MLU modernization, older F-16A/Bs were able to use the AIM-120 AMRAAM. However, the PAF had already received the AIM-9P/L Sidewinder and – unique among Viper operators – the French-made Magic 2 infrared-guided air-to-air missile. As well as US-made Paveway laser-guided bombs, Pakistani F-16s can use the French AS.30 laser-guided missile together with the French-made Atlis laser designator pod.

The PAF's F-16 fleet first saw combat during the Soviet war in Afghanistan, during which they responded to border violations by Soviet and Afghan aircraft. In the process, PAF F-16s were credited with shooting down at least eight intruders from Afghanistan between 1986 and 1988.

Since then, the PAF has repeatedly used its F-16s for airstrikes against Taliban and other insurgents in North-West Pakistan.

Border clashes

Pakistani F-16s have also been involved in some notable border clashes with the Indian Air Force. During an incident in February 2019, an IAF MiG-21 Bison fighter jet was shot down during a series of tit-for-tat aerial engagements, and its pilot was captured and later released. Pakistan denied that F-16s were involved in that incident, although India subsequently recovered and displayed wreckage of an AMRAAM missile, which suggests that a Viper was indeed responsible for the shootdown.

Singapore

Having transferred its surviving, older F-16A/B Block 15 OCU aircraft to Thailand, the Republic of Singapore Air Force (RSAF) operates some of the most sophisticated F-16 Fighting Falcons anywhere in the world, flying a total of 62 jets completed to F-16C/D Block 52 standard. Notably, these Block 52 aircraft are equipped with advanced Israeli-supplied equipment, including avionics, electronic warfare kit and weapons. In January 1985, under Peace Carvin I, Singapore ordered eight of the export-optimized F-16/79 aircraft, plus options for 12 more. Soon after, it became clear that the F100-powered F-16 would also be an option, and the contents of the

F-16D BLOCK 52

A Republic of Singapore Air Force (RSAF) Lockheed Martin F-16D Block 52, 679 (serial number 01-6028), 145 Squadron "Hornet", circa 2006. The 145 Squadron "Hornet" is a strike fighter squadron currently based at Changi Airbase (East).

eight-aircraft order were switched to F-16A/B Block 15 OCU aircraft (four single-seat F-16As and four two-seat F-16Bs).

Singapore received its first F-16 in February 1988. Initial deliveries were to Luke Air Force Base, Arizona, where a training squadron was established. Although the aircraft were from Block 15 production, they featured the strengthened Block 30 airframes. The first aircraft for the RSAF arrived in Singapore in January 1990. After the third Singaporean F-16 order, it was decided to dispose of the F-16A/Bs rather than upgrade them. In

December 2004, Singapore signed a deal with Thailand that provided for the transfer of the seven remaining F-16A/Bs.

Under Peace Carvin II, the RSAF first received the more advanced F-16C/D Block 52 aircraft. Plans to acquire 11 F-16C/Ds (five F-16Cs and six F-16Ds), plus two attrition replacements, were announced in 1993. By 1994, the order had been increased to 18 Block 52 aircraft (eight F-16Cs and 10 F-16Ds). These aircraft feature the F100-PW-229 engine, LANTIRN navigation and targeting pod and compatibility with AIM-120 AMRAAM and

F-16D Block 52	Range: 579km (360 miles)
Weight (maximum take-off): 19186.96kg (42,300lbs)	**Ceiling:** 16,764m (55,000ft)
	Crew: 2
Dimensions: Length 15.06m (49ft 5in), Wingspan 9.448m (31ft), Height 5.09m (16ft 8in)	**Armament:** One 20mm (0.787in) M61A1 six-barrel rotary cannon, plus up to 7700kg (17,000lb) of disposable stores carried
Powerplant: One Pratt & Whitney F100-PW-229 turbofan	on six hardpoints, including AGM-88 High-speed
Maximum speed: Mach 2.05	

AGM-88 HARM missiles. The first of the Peace Carvin II aircraft, an F-16D, was formally accepted by Singapore in April 1998 at Fort Worth. Deliveries to Singapore began in August of the same year.

As part of the RSAF training effort at Luke, Singapore also leased from Lockheed Martin 12 new-build F-16C/D Block 52 aircraft (four F-16Cs and eight F-16Ds), with options to purchase them later. With training on these aircraft continuing beyond the original two-and-a-half-year period of the lease, it seems likely that Singapore has bought these aircraft outright.

The third Singaporean F-16 Foreign Military Sale was Peace Carvin III, announced in October 1997 and covering another 12 F-16C/D Block 52 aircraft (10 F-16Cs and two F-16Ds). Deliveries took place between 2000 and 2002.

Most recently, the Peace Carvin IV deal, announced in July 2000, secured another 20 F-16 Block 52 aircraft for the RSAF. These comprised exclusively two-seat F-16Ds. Deliveries took place between 2003 and 2004.

The RSAF's two-seat F-16D Block 52 aircraft are unusual in that they feature the same kind of dorsal fairing as found on the Israeli F-16D Barak. Although unconfirmed, the housing is widely thought to accommodate the Israeli-supplied Elisra Advanced Self-Protection Suite (ASPS), which includes an SPS-3000 radar warning receiver and SPJ-40 radio frequency jammer.

Other Israeli equipment is understood to include Python 4 infrared-guided air-to-air missiles operated in conjunction with the Israeli DASH helmet-mounted sight. For anti-shipping strike, RSAF F-16C/Ds can be armed with US-supplied AGM-84 Harpoon missiles.

Taiwan

Taiwan's Republic of China Air Force (ROCAF) received a total of 150 F-16A/B Block 20 aircraft, delivered to a standard broadly equivalent to the MLU-upgraded jets. As well as upgrading the survivors from these deliveries, Taiwan has been approved to buy another 66 new-build F-16C/D Block 70 aircraft, mainly to counter the threat from mainland China.

In November 1992, the United States and Taiwan signed an agreement for the sale of 150 F-16A/B aircraft (120 F-16As and 30 F-16Bs) under the Peace Fenghuang (Peace Phoenix) Foreign Military Sales programme. The aircraft were completed to Block 15 OCU standards, with MLU specifications, but received the Block 20 production designation and are therefore unique to Taiwan. The deal reportedly cost around $6 billion, and the first five aircraft from Peace Fenghuang had been handed over by early 1997.

The Taiwanese Block 20 jets feature the AN/APG-66(V)3 radar that is compatible with AIM-7 Sparrow missiles and an advanced cockpit similar to that found in the Block 50 version. This includes night-vision-goggle compatibility, modular mission computer, GPS, colour multifunction displays and a wide-angle head-up display (HUD). All ROCAF F-16s are powered by F100-PW-220 engines.

In terms of armament and stores, the ROCAF F-16s were initially delivered with AIM-9M Sidewinder and AIM-7M Sparrow air-to-air missiles but can now also employ AIM-120 AMRAAMs and AGM-84 Harpoon anti-ship missiles. The jets can be fitted with AN/ALQ-184 electronic warfare pods, and they also use the Lockheed Martin Sharpshooter/Pathfinder navigation and targeting pods, which are export developments of the LANTIRN system. For reconnaissance, the F-16s use the AN/VDS-5 LOROP pod.

As part of ROCAF fighter modernization plans, the administration of US President Donald Trump in August 2019 approved the sale of an additional 66 new-build Block 70 F-16C/D jets to Taiwan. These jets are new production aircraft with a similar general configuration to the F-16V upgrade package. The first deliveries of these jets were expected to begin in 2023.

Originally, the ROCAF also expected to receive 144 F-16Vs, produced as conversions of its existing F-16A/B jets. However, this number has since been reduced to 141 through attrition in its existing Viper fleet.

Lockheed Martin upgraded the first two ROCAF F-16Vs, the first of which took to the air in October 2015, and these served as pattern aircraft for Taiwan's Aerospace Industry Development Center (AIDC) to complete the remaining upgrades locally.

The F-16V brings with it a host of new weapons capabilities, including the AIM-9X Sidewinders,

TAIWANESE F-16
A Republic of China Air Force (ROCAF) F-16 jet fighter takes off from Chiashan Air Force Base, August 2004. The aircraft was test-firing US-made Harpoon anti-ship missiles in a display of the island's ability to ward off a Chinese seaborne invasion.

while it also offers compatibility with the GBU-31/38 Joint Direct Attack Munition (JDAM), GBU-54/56 Laser JDAM, CBU-105 Sensor Fused Weapon, AGM-88 High-speed Anti-Radiation Missile (HARM), AGM-154 Joint Standoff Weapon (JSOW) and AGM-84H Standoff Land Attack Missile-

Expanded Response (SLAM-ER). Transfer of the HARM, JSOW and SLAM-ER weapons was approved by the US State Department in separate deals in 2017 and 2020.

Upgrade F16Vs

While the F-16V name is applied almost universally to these aircraft,

AIDC refers to them as F-16A/B Block 20 MLUs.

In November 2021, Taiwan officially introduced to service its first wing of upgraded F-16Vs, at Chiayi Air Base in the southwest of the country. According to reports, 64 of the jets had been upgraded by this point.

South American Operators

Venezuela was the first Latin American nation to be approved to buy the F-16 and remained the only user in the South American continent until it was joined by Chile more than two decades later. The status of the Venezuelan F-16 fleet has long been precarious, ever since Hugo Chávez became president and the country established close relationships (including military) with China and Russia. The same policy continued under Chávez's successor, Nicolás Maduro, with the United States blocking any further weapons sales to Caracas. Despite this, the Venezuelan Air Force manages to retain its F-16 fleet in an operational condition, albeit at a very low state of readiness.

VENEZUELAN F-16

A Venezuelan Air Force F-16 manoeuvres during Cruzex III at the Anapolis Air Base, Brazil, August 2006, during joint exercises. More than 1700 personnel and 90 aircraft from six countries – Argentina, Chile, Uruguay, Venezuela, Brazil and France – participated in the operation.

Venezuela

The F-16 fleet of the Venezuelan Air Force – officially, the Aviación Militar Bolivariana Venezolana (AMBV, or Bolivarian Venezuelan Military Aviation) – dates to the Peace Delta programme of the 1980s, which provided Venezuela with 16 single-seat F-16As and eight two-seat F-16Bs. All aircraft were completed to Block 15 standards. At one point, it had been expected that Venezuela would receive the export-optimized F-16/79 version with the J79 engine, but Washington eventually approved the standard F-16A/B with the F100 powerplant.

After a Foreign Military Sales agreement signed in May 1982, the jets were delivered between 1983 and 1985, together with 150 AIM-9L/P-4 Sidewinder AAMs. Once in service, the new fighters replaced the older Mirage III interceptors and Mirage 5 ground-attack aircraft.

At one stage, prior to the collapse of relations with the United States, Venezuela was looking to increase its F-16 fleet by acquiring a small number of aircraft as attrition replacements.

At the same time, Caracas planned to upgrade its 22 surviving aircraft, including with the introduction of F100-PW-220E engines. Such planes were approved by the United States in late 1997 but were never followed through.

F-16B Block 15T

Weight (maximum take-off): 17,010kg (37,500lbs) empty, 11467.27kg (25,281lbs) combat, 17009.71kg (37,500lbs) maximum takeoff

Dimensions: Length 15.14m (49ft 8in); Wingspan 9.97m (32ft 8in); Height 4.9m (16ft 1in)

Powerplant: One Pratt & Whitney F100-PW-220 turbofan

Maximum speed: 1472.55km/h (915mph) at sea level

Range: 1166.77km (725 miles)

Ceiling: 6598.92m (21,650ft)

Crew: 2

Armament: One M61A1 20mm (0.787in) cannon; six hardpoints

Opposite: **F-16A BLOCK 15**
This F-16A wears the characteristic markings of Venezuela. Twenty-four F-16As were delivered to the two squadrons of Grupo de Caza 16 at Maracay, wearing scrambled serials to confuse observers. Air defence is their main mission although air-to-ground operations are also important, hence the camouflage.

Below: **VENEZUELAN F-16B BLOCK 15T**
A General Dynamics F-16B Block 15T, 9583 (serial number 83-1191), flying with Group 16, Venezuelan Air Force.

F-16A Block 15

Weight (maximum take-off): 17,010kg (37,500lbs)

Dimensions: Length 15.01m (49ft 3.5in); Wingspan 9.995m (32ft 9.5in); Height 5.09m (16ft 8.5in)

Powerplant: One Pratt & Whitney F100-PW-220 turbofan

Maximum speed: Mach 2.05 at 40,000ft

Range: 3862km (2400 miles)

Ceiling: 16,764m (55,000ft)

Crew: 1

Armament: One 20mm (0.787in) M61A1 six-barrel rotary cannon, plus six hardpoints

The surviving Venezuelan F-16s continue to serve with the Grupo Aéreo de Caza No 16 'Los Dragones', based at El Libertador, in Maracay, in the centre of the country. The Venezuelan F-16s have been modified to use the Israeli-made Python 4 air-to-air missile, supplementing the AIM-9L. Other weapons options include 226.8kg (500 lb) Mk 82 and 907.2kg (2,000 lb) Mk 84 unguided bombs, cluster bombs and rockets. Israel has also provided Venezuela with the Litening navigation and targeting pod, and it may also have received Israeli-made precision-guided air-to-ground weapons in recent years.

Venezuelan F-16s flew missions during the military coup launched against President Carlos Andres Perez in November 1992.

Chile

The Chilean Air Force – or Fuerza Aérea de Chile (FACh) – operates one of the most potent fighter fleets anywhere in Latin America, with the F-16 very much at the forefront. The FACh's status as a leading regional air power began in the late 1980s, with a modernization programme driven by the country's improving economic situation and by rivalries with its three neighbours: Argentina, Bolivia and Peru.

CHILEAN F-16
A Chilean Air Force F-16C lands at Parnamirim, Brazil, during joint exercises.

121

F-16D Block 50

Weight (maximum take-off): 19,186.96kg (42,300lbs)

Dimensions: Length 15.06m (49ft 5in), Wingspan 9.448m (31ft), Height 5.09m (16ft 8in)

Powerplant: One Pratt & Whitney F100-PW-229 turbofan

Maximum speed: Mach 2.05

Range: 579km (360 miles)

Ceiling: 16,764m (55,000ft)

Crew: 2

Armament: One 20mm (0.787in) M61A1 six-barrel rotary cannon, plus six hardpoints

In late 2000, after a long process to select a new fighter aircraft, Chile announced that it would acquire 10 examples of the F-16C/D Block 50 as part of a programme known locally as Caza 2000 (Fighter 2000). The option to buy US-made fighters had long been off the table because of the political situation in South America. However, in 1997, Washington had permitted Lockheed Martin to offer the F-16 as part of a liberalized arms sales policy in the region.

In May 2002, Lockheed Martin announced the signature of the $320 million Peace Puma Foreign Military Sales contract covering six single-seat F-16Cs and four two-seat F-16Ds for the FACh. The first Chilean Fighting Falcon made its maiden flight on 23 June 2005, and deliveries began in March 2006. The Block 50 jets equipped the unit at Iquique in the north of the country.

Expanded fleet

After introducing the Block 50 jets, Chile then decided to increase its F-16 fleet, primarily to enable the replacement of the ageing Dassault Mirage 5 Elkan. After negotiations

CHILEAN F-16D BLOCK 50M
A Lockheed Martin F-16D Block 50M, 859 (serial number 02-6038), from the Grupo de Aviación n°3 (FACh), Chilean Air Force. The first F-16 was delivered to the squadron in 2006, replacing the existing F-5E and Mirage VM.

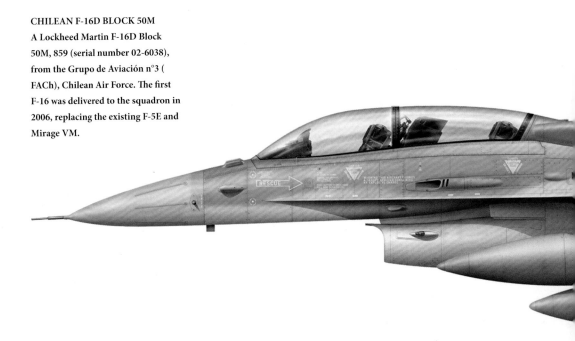

that began in late 2004, a batch of 18 second-hand F-16A/B Block 20 aircraft (11 single-seaters and seven two-seaters) were purchased from the Netherlands. A contract valued at $185 million was signed in late 2005, and deliveries began in November 2006. Prior to delivery, the former Dutch jets had all passed through the MLU programme, but they remain less sophisticated than Chile's F-16C/D aircraft. The first batch of former Dutch jets, acquired under the Peace Amstel I programme, entered service at Antofagasta (also in the north of Chile).

More F-16s were then sought by Chile as the process of replacing the FACh's Mirage fleet continued. Once again, the Netherlands would be the source of the second-hand jets, supplanting the Mirage 50 Pantera, which had been withdrawn in late 2007. The same year, an offer was received from the Netherlands, again covering 18 F-16 Block 20 aircraft, all single-seaters, worth up to $160 million. The first six aircraft under the Peace Amstel II programme were delivered by the end of 2010. Originally intended to be based at Punta Arenas in the far south

of the country, it was found that the F-16 was not best suited to the difficult conditions at the base, where rocks are regularly blown onto the runway. Instead, the Peace Amstel II jets were introduced to service at Antofagasta.

Israeli armament
Unusually, Chile's F-16C/Ds are armed with Israeli-made Rafael Python 4 and Derby air-to-air missiles as well as US-made weapons, and they are also capable of using Joint Direct Attack Munition (JDAM) precision-guided bombs.

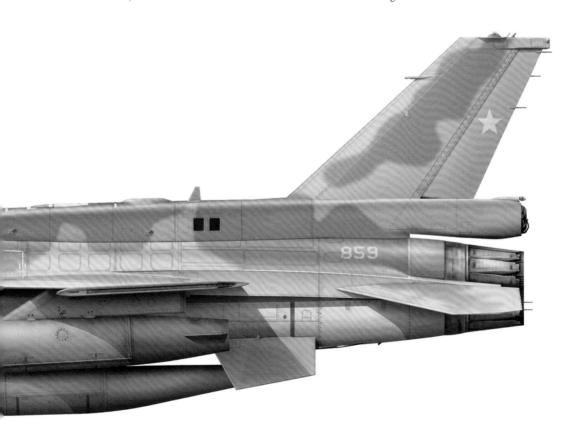

Index

References to illustration and photo captions in **bold**.

Picture Credits

Alamy: 15 (NB/ROD), 62/63 & 91 & 102/103 (Stocktrek Images), 117 (Associated Press)

Dreamstime: 34/35 (VanderWolfImages), 81 (Berkaviation), 85 (Evrenkalinbacak), 89 (Caspar107)

Getty Images: 12 (Bettmann), 13 (Dirck Halstead), 14 (Avalon), 56 (Universal Images Group), 115 (Patrick Lin/AFP)

NASA: 17 (Dryden Flight Research Center), 18 (Lewis Research Center), 19, 33 & 39 (Dryden Flight Research Center)

Shutterstock: 86 (Emilio100), 87 (VanderWolf Images), 105 (vaalaa), 108 (Gilang Putraditya Purba), 110 (twintyre), 120/121 (Artejose)

U.S. Air Force: 7 (Christian Turner), 8 (Mike Killian), 9 (Samuel King), 11 (SSgt Cecilio Ricardo Jr), 21, 22, 23, 32 (SSgt Shannon Collins),

37 (SRA Greg L Davis), 38 (Major Matthew Mutti), 42/43 (MSgt Andrew Moseley), 50 (TSgt Michael Ammons), 59 (TSgt Emerson Nunez), 65 (SrA Joshua Hoskins), 66 (MSgt Dean Kuhlman), 67 (MSgt Michael Ammons), 68 (SrA Jeffrey Allen), 72/73 (SSgt Lee F Corkran), 75 (SSgt Jason Robertson), 80 (MSgt Andy Dunaway), 98 (MSgt Kevin Gruenwald), 101 (TSgt Michael R Holzworth)

U.S. Department of Defense: 16, 40, 55

ARTWORKS
Amber Books: 24, 28–31, 48/49, 77, 82, 97, 106, 119

Rolando Ugolini: 5, 25, 26, 40, 41, 44–47, 57, 58, 60/61, 76, 78, 79, 83, 84, 88, 92–95, 99, 100, 107, 109, 112/113, 118, 122/123

Teasel Studios: 51, 52–53, 70–71